Building a Log Cabin in Alaska in Four Months

Using the trees from two acres of land

By Charles (Woody) Underwood

Bonus: Building a Pergola Patio Cover

ISBN: 9780615640211 (eBook)

ISBN: 9781469943473 (Print)

DEDICATION

Special thanks to my wonderful wife Su.

CONTENTS

PREFACE

This book should be helpful as a "how to" guide for a man working alone to build a strong, yet simple log cabin made to last. It can be a log cabin that a man can be proud to call his home or for a getaway home on the weekend. I built the 13 by 41 foot cabin shell, including cutting down the trees and peeling off the bark, in three months while camping out in a tent. Cutting down the trees and peeling off the bark took more than half of the time in completing the shell of the cabin. It was hard work, but by using the trees on my property, and a couple that I got off the river's gravel bar, I saved money and it gave me a more satisfying feeling of accomplishment as I lived my dream. I did the work myself without anyone or any heavy log moving equipment helping. My wife, Su, and my then seven year old son Anthony helped me to work on the cabin mainly by freeing me from having to cook, clean, and do other daily chores while the cabin went up. We lived in a tent on our property for 4½ months as we built the cabin. The extra month and a half was needed due to the not expected deep snow upon our arrival in March in Alaska, and having to survey the land before I could start cutting down trees. I give some special pointers that will help with building a log cabin in a cold, snowy place like Alaska, but most of what I write can be used to build a log cabin in a forested area anywhere. After three months' work the cabin shell was up and we moved from our tents into the cabin, however, the well and plumbing, septic system, woodstove &

chimney, interior walls, electrical wiring, and 8 by 28 foot add-on to the side of the cabin, which are covered in varying details (less on the wiring and plumbing) in this book, were worked on as I got the time and money. Overall, to complete the cabin, it took about four to five months of my time. The 757 square foot cabin was completed in about four months' time working long hours, six days a week. The long camping experience was an ordeal for my wife, but my son and I enjoyed it. We thank God for His help and guidance through it all. The plans contained in this book are designed to allow a man working alone to build a cabin in a short time that will last a life time. I include an additional chapter about building a pergola type patio cover out of red cedar. 59 pictures are included in this book. I built the log cabin in 1992 but my first trip to Alaska was in 1981 when I went there looking for adventure and prospecting for gold. I wrote about that experience in the book: THE WILD STILL CALLS TO ALASKA: Looking for gold; enjoying the wild!

1   FINDING THE RIGHT LAND

There are several things to consider when buying land. If you don't plan on buying the logs, then there must be enough trees of the right size and type on your land to cut into logs for your cabin. We had enough trees growing on our 1¾ acre (7082 m²) lot to build our cabin, the add-on, two storage sheds, a wood shed, and to have firewood for 3½ years with still enough trees left standing for pleasant scenery. I do wish, however, that I had had more of the larger 12 inch (30.5 cm) diameter trees on our land to use to build the cabin. Trees larger than 12 inch (30.5 cm) in diameter are very heavy and hard to move if longer than 8 feet (2.44 meters) in length. White spruce was the main tree that I used, but I also used birch, aspen, and tamarack. I used treated lumber for my foundation where it touched the ground, but if you decide to use untreated logs touching the ground use something rot resistant like white spruce or cedar (juniper). It is important to use treated lumber or cement for a permanent cabin's foundation. Buying the logs already cut down and debarked should take about 7-8 weeks off of your building time. The bought logs not only add a lot to the cost, they also do not have the draw knife look or add as much to the satisfaction of working the trees into a log house by your own skill and efforts. Even so, it is a lot easier and faster using bought logs and you are nevertheless still building your own log cabin. Just not from scratch.

Another thing to consider is permafrost. It is best not to build on permafrost land. Land with permafrost has smaller trees growing on it, and it moves and heaves each year as it thaws and freezes. Permafrost is ground that, even during the summer, remains frozen about 4 or 5 feet (1.22 or 1.52 m) below the surface of the ground. Most of the interior of Alaska has discontinuous permafrost. This is ground that is frozen in patches. The problem with permafrost is that if it is in dirt or clay and not gravel, then, if it unthaws, your cabin will most likely sink or settle uneven. So it is best not to buy land that has permafrost on it, but if you do, it should at least have gravel 1-4 feet (0.3-1.22 m) below the top soil and not clay type soil which holds a lot of water. Once the trees, which shade the ground, are removed, and a cabin that is heated is built, the permafrost can start to melt. I will go into more detail about permafrost in the chapters to come.

If you plan on building near a river, it would be best to look at the land during spring break up in May or June when the river is flooding and in the rainy season in your area. On most rivers and creeks you should be at least 15 feet (4.6 m) above the normal river level. But on many rivers 15 or even 30 feet (4.6 or 9.1 m) would not be enough for the so called 100 or 500 year floods. Where we lived, I was planning on building on a certain section of our property which would have been closer to where the electric power lines run by. But, thank God, the river rose to flood stage before I started building. There is a levee in between our property and the river; so when the river rose up higher than our property, but lower than the levee, springs of water flowed up from under the levee in low places. The springs made a slow flowing creek about ½ a foot (15.2 cm) deep and 75 feet (23 m) wide across the lower part of our property where I had first considered building the cabin. Instead, I built the cabin on the highest ground on our property, which was a gravel bar. The gravel bar was formed hundreds of years ago when the river had changed course and ran through there. It now has about 1 foot (0.3 m) of top soil and several large trees growing on it.

Some people express interest in getting a free homestead in Alaska. Homesteading in Alaska is not what it used to be in the 1960's and earlier. The BLM has not offered land for homesteading since 1986. If they did, in order to qualify for the so called "free" land, one has to first live in Alaska for one whole year first to be eligible. The Bureau of Land Management (BLM) can give you more details. It is my understanding that none of the land that was made available near the end of the program in 1986 could be accessed by road. Air, boat, or trail access creates extra problems and expenses. The state of Alaska has sometimes sold small portions of land for remote recreational cabin use. The Alaska Department of Natural Resources would have information about any upcoming land sales, but do not expect any bargains.

2   WHEN TO MOVE, WHAT TO EXPECT, AND HELPFUL IDEAS

Alaska's weather can be very unpredictable. Our first spring here, while we were camping in tents, was very cold. In March and April it got down to negative 15 Fahrenheit (-26 Celsius) on several nights and down to 29 degrees Fahrenheit below zero (-34 Celsius) on April the 13th (setting a record for that day in Fairbanks at -23 Fahrenheit (-31 Celsius)). If it wasn't extremely cold, then it was snowing. We got about 2½ feet (0.762 meters) of snow during our first spring in Alaska's interior of which 14 inches (35.56 cm) fell in May setting a record that year for Fairbanks. Our gravel road, which is a little over ¼ of a mile (402 meters) long, got snowed in. It took me two days of very hard work to hand shovel the entire road clear enough to drive out. The good part about it was that it helped to keep me in shape for cutting and dragging logs. The second spring was just the opposite. It was the second warmest spring on record at that time and snowed less than 5 inches (12.7 cm). When the spring is colder than normal, then the river ice doesn't break up until the very last. When this happens, the ice then goes out all at once making a spectacular break up with flooding. Some snow is usually on the ground in the shaded wooded areas from the last of April until the middle of May depending on the weather. I arrived in Alaska on March the 25th in 1992 to discover that ninety percent of the winter's snow was still on the ground and more was coming. There was still snow in the shady areas into the first week of June our first year there.

Something else to consider are the mosquitoes. The mosquito is jokingly referred to as Alaska's state bird. May and June are the two worse months for mosquitoes. In order to save money, instead of using bug repellent, I wore a fine mesh net over a cowboy type straw hat, and I wore a long sleeve shirt. A baseball cap covered with a net will work as well. Some areas have more mosquitoes than others. If the mosquitoes swarm you in August or September, then I recommend finding some other area to live because they will probably carry you away in June when they are at their peak. Each year the number of mosquitoes can vary from a few to a lot depending on the weather and other things like the number of hornets around which eat the mosquitoes.

I found that the least expensive way of moving all of our belongings up to Alaska from Texas was to use a 16 foot (4.88 meter) flatbed trailer, and cover everything with a tarp. I used the cheap plastic tarp to cover everything. In the wind the plastic tarp whips and tears. To prevent this, I attached several ropes across the tarp to hold it down. I also checked the tarp often and used duct tape to repair tears before they got worse. A good cloth tarp would have been better. When we moved back to Texas in January of 2002, I built an enclosure for the trailer out of ½ inch (1.27 cm) plywood sheets and 2" x 4" (5.1 cm x 10.2 cm) boards. I screwed 1½ to 1¾ inch (3.8 to 4.45 cm) wood screws through the plywood and into the 2" x 4" (5.1 cm x 10.2 cm) boards where the 4' x 8' (1.22 x 2.44 m) plywood sheets met up. I even made a plywood roof by adding 2" x 2" x 8' (5.1 x 5.1 cm x 2.44 m) boards around the top edge of the plywood "wall" boards. I sealed the seams (plywood to plywood edge joints) with 2" x 4" (5.1 x 10.2 cm) boards. Very little rain can get in through these joints, but you can caulk the joints up to help even more if you wish using a flexible caulk like silicone. I packed our belongings in water proof trash bags to keep water and dust off our stuff. I used barrels for some things, but round barrels do not pack as tightly as square boxes do.

The road to Alaska through Canada is called "The Alaskan Highway". It runs from Dawson Creek in British Colombia Canada to Delta Junction in Alaska a distance of 1422 miles (2289 km). From there you have 96 miles (155 km) to reach Fairbanks, Alaska (the unofficial end of the Alaskan highway). "The Milepost" is a good book and map combination for good detail and advice for traveling the Alaskan Highway. The Alaskan Highway is great now. When I first drove up it in 1981 it was mostly gravel and I wore out several tires on the journey back. My truck was heavily loaded and the gravel ate my tires up. I have driven the Alaskan Highway 9 times with 2002 being my last time as of this writing. Make sure you have good tires on your truck and trailer. Don't forget the spare tire for both the truck and the trailer. Flat fixer plugs are good to have. It is wise to carry flares, battery jumper cables, and a fire extinguisher as well. Driving the Alaskan highway for the first time is an adventure of a sort by its self. Enjoy the ride!

3 LIVING IN A TENT FOR FOUR AND ONE HALF MONTHS

I mentioned in the last chapter that we arrived in Alaska on March the 25th and found ninety percent of the snow still on the ground with 2½ feet (0.76 m) more to come. The gravel road that goes by our property was not used during the winter due to no one living back there. I hired a man with a backhoe loader to remove the snow along the gravel road which goes toward our property. At that time I didn't know for sure exactly where our land was. But, thank God; I unknowingly had the man to stop clearing the road of snow in a little clearing which actually ended up being on our own property. Due to the snow and needing to survey the land, I wasn't able to start building right away. Despite the snow still covering the ground, I started cutting down trees and dragging and stacking them in a central location the last of April which was about one month after we had arrived.

When we first arrived, I set up four tents. Two tents, about 6½ feet by 6½ feet (2 x 2 m) were used for storing our belongings which were taken from off the trailer. Another tent, about 6½ feet by 6½ feet (2 x 2 m), was used for our kitchen and eating area. It had a table in it on which we placed the stove. At first we used a Coleman unleaded gasoline stove. It worked well for us, but later on I bought a propane gas stove that hooked up to a 30 pound (13.6 kg) propane tank. It was much more convenient to use. I had two 30 pound (13.6 kg) tanks to use with it. Even though the tent had a screened in roof to ventilate and let the heat out, for safety reasons (carbon dioxide and fire dangers) I can't recommend using a stove inside a tent as we did. A nylon tent will burn very fast once set on fire. Cotton canvas tents are safer. We sat beside the table on lawn chairs and propped our feet up off the frozen ground to keep them warmer.

Our sleeping tent, which also held some supplies, was 7 by 12 feet (2.13 x 3.66 m). We slept on cots, which not only added comfort but also kept us off the cold ground. When it was coldest, we slept in two sleeping bags. I put a good 5 pound (2.3 kg) Quallofil filled mummy style sleeping bag, which is rated to -10 F (-23.3 C) degrees, inside of a 4 pound (1.8 kg) Hollofil filled square bag. These were placed on top of wool blankets with one wool blanket placed over the top of the sleeping bags. At first I used a foam rubber pad below our blankets on top of the cot. I found that the moisture from our body would pass through the sleeping bags and blankets but would stop and form a layer of ice at the rubber mat so I removed them. We slept in polypropylene long Johns, jeans and a cotton shirt, down cover all pants, a woolly pulley sweater, a wool jacket, and a good down parka rated to -70 F (-57 C) degrees. We wore wool stretchable stocking hats on our heads and covered our faces with an acrylic scarf. We wore wool socks on our feet along with the wool insert booties from Pac boots. We wore oversized mittens (they are a little over 1 foot long (30 cm)) on our hands. My seven year old boy and I always slept warm even when it got down to -29 F (-33.9 C) degrees (without any heat in the tent). But my wife, as women often do, has poor circulation in her feet so they would get cold at night. When we would change from our Pac boots into dry wool socks and wool booties at night to go to bed, both my feet and my boy's would steam up in the cold air, but my wife's feet weren't warm enough to steam up much. I ended up getting her some bunny boots to sleep in, which helped a little more. Bunny boots are the insulated rubber boots rated to negative 70 F (-57 C) degrees which the military used at one time. We didn't use any heat to keep warm in our tents. Every morning, while it was cold, I would put on insulated rubber gloves and scrape the ice crystals that formed from our breath off the ceiling of the tent into a plastic bowl because when the sun came up, its heat melted the ice crystals and they would drip on our beds.

We took baths once a week by standing in a 2 foot square (0.19 sq. m) galvanized wash tub inside of the kitchen tent. We used a plastic glass to pour warm water over us. At first it was too cold to take that type of bath so we cleaned up with just a hot wash cloth instead.

Soon after arriving, I had to cut a hole in the river ice in order to have drinking water. We lived by the Salcha River, which is a clear running river. I have been told that even silty rivers like the Tanana run clear during the winter when under ice since the glaziers stop grinding the rocks during the winter. Anyway, I tied a rope around a tree to carry with me in case I broke through the ice; I am from Texas where rivers rarely freeze. I shoveled the snow off the land until I reached the river ice. I continued forward shoveling the snow off and testing the strength of the river ice until I felt I had gone far enough out. I then used a heavy iron rod with a chisel end to pick a hole through the ice. The Salcha River flows fast there, so the ice was only about 6 inches (15 cm) thick at that time. We kept getting our water from the river until it became too dirty to drink during the ice break up. It flows dirty for about two months each year when the ice breaks up and the river floods. There are several water filters made for camping purposes that are easy to use to insure safer drinking water or you can boil the water. I did not know about the convenient water filters at that time and boiling water takes too long so we just drank the water from the river. I was unaware of how dangerous Beaver Fever (Giardiasis) can be. To prevent the hole from freezing over, you can cover it with sticks and cardboard and then put snow on top of it so the ice will not freeze up as much for the next time. Some laundry mats have water for sale or even free if you wash your clothes there. My wife washed our clothes by hand in a wash tub over a wash board in order to save money while we were in the tents until the river became dirty during break up. I thought it would not only save us money, but would be a good experience for her to live like the pioneers of old did. Even I had to wash my clothes by hand while in boot camp in the Marines & I was the one who hauled the water up from the river for her to use. She told me that I should use an axe instead of a chainsaw to cut down trees and build the cabin so I could experience what the pioneers went through as well. I told her that winter is coming and that it would take too long using an axe without a chainsaw.

In order to save money we ate low cost foods. For breakfast we ate oatmeal or homemade pancakes. For lunch we ate homemade tortillas with butter and honey, pinto beans, rice, and after it warmed up enough, one can of vegetables, usually spinach. For supper we had the same and added Chinese Ramen noodles for a snack at night. We got so tired of eating pinto and large Lima "butter" beans that we splurged and bought canned pork and beans toward the last. Still beans and inexpensive but different tasting.

Here is our bean & rice recipe that we use. I like to use 5 cups of beans & 1 cup of rice mixed together after cooking both separately. In freezing temperatures you can omit the fresh vegetables and can tomatoes. In order to get the proper protein and amino acids that meat contains it is important to have either beans & rice or beans & corn together. I like using a pressure cooker to cook the beans.

<u>Pressure Cooker Beans</u> (4 cups of pinto or other type beans) or use 5 cups of beans and slightly increase the seasonings.

1) Rinse & presoak 8 to 12 hours covered with water.

2) Drain off water and recover with fresh water.

3) Add the following:

1 Tablespoon of olive oil (controls foaming)

5 cloves of garlic (chopped)

1 onion (chopped)

1 jalapeno pepper (fresh) + (chopped)

2 Tablespoons of chili powder

1 Tablespoon of cumin powder

1 Tablespoon garlic powder

1 teaspoon cayenne pepper (optional if no fresh jalapeno pepper)

1 teaspoon salt

2 teaspoons black pepper

4) Heat on high (10) until starts to jiggle then turn down to medium low (3.7) and cook for 40 minutes. If you double the recipe still cook it for 40 minutes. I found that 5 cups of beans & mixed with 1 cup of rice works well.

<u>Brown (whole grain) Rice</u>:

1 cup brown rice

2 cups water

½ teaspoon salt

1 teaspoon each of cumin, oregano, garlic powder, curry (all optional)

1 green bell peppers chopped (optional)

1 can of Ro-tel diced tomatoes & green chilies (optional)

INSTRUCTIONS: Place rice and everything in a medium saucepan and bring to a boil over high heat (10). After it starts to boil cover with a tight fitting lid, and reduce the heat to low (1.6). Simmer covered undisturbed until the rice is tender, about 50 minutes. Remove from heat and let sit covered to steam for 10 minutes more. Fluff with a fork and serve. Do not lift lid to look during the whole process. Mix beans and rice together and enjoy!

We placed a portable toilet, which is made to go by the side of a handicapped person's bed, inside one of our storage tents. We used plastic trash bags to prevent clean up problems. You can't dig cat holes to bury waste in the frozen dirt, and I wouldn't want to for four and one half months anyway. We still used this system until I put in a septic tank with a flush toilet. It's a lot warmer in the house on a portable potty in the winter than our outhouse is. We used wet baby wipes to clean our hands. To urinate during the night, instead of leaving the tent, we used large plastic juice jars. Women can use a large flexible plastic glass and then pour it into the jar. We cleaned the glass and jar with bleach and water every day.

If you buy the type of tent that doesn't have a rain fly, then you should use a plastic tarp over the tent. If you arrive during the winter like we did, then bring or buy a snow shovel. If it is snowing heavily you can wipe the snow off the tent with a broom. One of our tents collapsed due to too much snow a couple of times.

Getting water from Salcha River through the ice

Getting water from Salcha River through the ice near break up

Our camp

Doing the laundry by hand

Snowshoeing near camp surveying

Showing winter parka gear & our dog (1994)

Us three & Salcha River

4 TOOLS

The main tool you will need is a <u>chain saw</u>. For the main cabin, I used a Husqvarna 45 which has a 2.75 cubic inch (0.046 liter) engine. Husqvarna is nicknamed "Husky". It has an 18 inch (46 cm) long bar. I found it to be a good saw for cutting trees and working them on the ground. It was a little heavy for lifting up to cut the beams' mortise and tenon joints. Overall, however, I recommend the Husqvarna 45 chain saw. On the add-on I used a different chainsaw, the Homelite, which has a 2.0 cubic inch (0.033 liter) engine. It has an 18 inch (46 cm) long blade. It is lighter than the Husky, which made it less tiresome to hold up, but it took longer to cut logs into shape due to the smaller engine. The Homelite is an inexpensive saw compared with the Husky, but it still performed well for what I was using it for. Having an extra backup chainsaw might come in handy if one should have problems or get the bar pinched or stuck while making a cut. The chain saw will need the flat and rat tail file <u>sharpening kit</u> as well. Note: most new chain saws have a spark arrester screen at the exhaust muffler to help prevent forest fires. This screen will usually clog up with carbon and cause the saw to lose power. You will need to clean the screen once this happens. I removed mine entirely.

You will need a drawknife to peel the bark off the logs. I would cut down two or three trees, cut them into the rough lengths I needed, and haul them to a central location to peel the bark off. I used a curved drawknife for this. It is a little harder to sharpen than a straight drawknife blade but worked best for me. I used 18 inch (46 cm) long files to sharpen it. Put the drawknife in a vise clamp and file with a medium file and then a fine file. File evenly on one side only. Don't remove small limbs or knots with the drawknife; use an axe for that first. The axe can also be used to remove the bark from trees much faster than a drawknife once the sap starts flowing. Just cut a strip of bark off on one side using the axe. Then use the axe blade to pry up some of the remaining bark to get the axe head in between the log and bark. Then start working the bark off by pulling the axe away from the log along with the bark. This process is faster and easier than using a drawknife, but it does leave a very thin inner layer of bark and you will not have the drawknife blade cuts in the log.

You will need two hammers: a regular hammer to drive nails and a heavier hammer to drive spikes. You will need a sledge hammer to drive rebar with. A one inch wide chisel will be needed to make recesses for the hinges. A doorknob hole cutter for the doors.

I did most of my work by eye, without a level, but you can use a level. Since logs are not square, you can use a plumb bob with a string tied to it and placed at the top of the wall to help determine the squareness of the wall in relation to the floor. This is hard to do so I just "eyed" the wall logs to be standing square with the floor. Some string tied to stakes can be useful to mark off where the cabin will go. A string level is a level which has little hooks on it to connect onto a string. Hopefully you can choose a spot to build that is level, but if not, the string level can help you determine what height is needed for your piers across the distance of your cabin so that it will have a level flat floor. Measuring a triangle with 6 by 8 feet (1.8288 x 2.4384 meters) for the 90 degree corner and with 10 feet (3.048 meters) measured across the other end to join it together can be used to check for a square corner. Some use a compass for getting a rough lay out to get the corners square. Due to working with irregular shaped logs, I just used my eye to square things up. I found that using a tape measure to keep lengths and heights all the same was more important and helpful.

I didn't use them, but a log mover and carrier tools don't cost much and it makes moving logs easier. Since my vertical wall logs were only 8 feet (2.44 m) long, I wrapped an old jacket around the log and dragged it. The old jacket helped to keep tree sap off my clothes and to protect them from the rough bark. On the bigger diameter sill logs I tied a six foot long sturdy pole onto the log with a ¼ inch (0.64 cm) nylon rope and kind of rowed the log along the ground to where I wanted it. The debarked logs dried enough to be much lighter when it came time to use them in building the cabin during the fewer than two months' time that they sat in the stack. A hand drill with a 1½ foot (0.46 m) long, ½ inch (1.3 cm) diameter drill bit is needed to make holes for the rebar and to pre-drill holes for the spikes that go into the plate logs. You will need a 25 and 100 foot (7.6 + 30 meter) long tape measures, a shovel, a narrow spade, and a posthole digger. After the shell of the cabin is completed other specialty tools will be needed for the electric wiring, well, plumbing, sewer, sheet rocked walls, and other things.

5 BASIC PLANS FOR CABIN SHELL

It is important to know what size and shape cabin you plan to build before you start cutting down trees. Your biggest diameter trees should be used for the sill logs. The plate and wall logs would be next, and the ridgepole then the joist and beams could be smaller in diameter. Keeping in mind what you will be using the logs for will help you to cut the amount and lengths needed for your cabin with less waste of logs and time cutting them. I will give you my plans for a cabin 13 by 41 feet (3.96 x 12.5 m), and then the add-on of 8 by 28 feet (2.44 x 8.53 m). If you use 6-inch (15.2 cm) diameter logs, then you will need about 190 8-fcct (2.44 m) long wall logs. If you use 8-inch (20.3 cm) diameter logs, then you will need about 160 8-feet (2.44 m) long wall logs. Stack the wall logs into a separate pile from the other logs to make it easier to keep up with where you are at with what you will need. The larger diameter the log, the greater the insulation value the logs will have. There is supposed to be about a 1½ R-value per inch (2.54 cm) of log thickness. Logs do better about retaining their heat than fiberglass does. Logs have a good U-value. A U-value is the measure of rate of heat loss through a material.

Sill logs run along the outside bottom edge of the cabin and are the base for the wall logs. Unless you have some help moving heavy logs around you will need several shorter length sill logs. (Note that I used these lengths of sill, plate, and ridge pole logs so that I could handle their weight while working alone. If you have help then you can go with longer length logs.) Sill logs should be 12 inches (30.5 cm) in diameter. With the main cabin being 13 x 41 feet (3.96 x 12.5 m) I used eight 9-footers (2.74 m), four 8-footers (2.44 m), and four 3-footers (0.91 m) for the sill logs. For your sill and plate logs, you can go with longer logs if you can handle carrying the added weight or have someone helping you. I used these lengths so I could handle the weight of the logs working by myself. For the floor joist you will need thirty-one 12¼ feet long (3.73 m), 6-inch (15.2 cm) diameter logs. They will be placed one every 16 inches (40.64 cm) apart. (Note: I used smaller in diameter joist than this and had to strengthen to floor so it would be sturdier). You will also need thirty-one 5-6 inch (13-15 cm) diameter, 12¼ feet (3.73 m) long beams which are also spaced every 16 inches (40.6 cm) apart. You will need some plate logs to go across the top of the wall logs. For the plate logs you can use ten 8-footers (2.44 m), two 9 footers (2.74 m), and two 13 footers (3.96 m) of at least 8 inches (20.3 cm) diameter, but preferably 10 inches (25.4 cm) diameter. In between the beam and the ridge pole are some 2½ feet (0.76 m) long posts which hold the ridge pole up above the beams. You will need thirty-three posts at 5 inch (13 cm) diameter each. Precut these at 2 feet 9 inches (0.8 m); then recut to fit when installing. (Note: you can use shorter than 2½ feet (0.76 m) if you want less pitch or slope on your roof). The ridge pole runs the length of the cabin across the top and extends beyond the cabin on both ends about 2 feet (0.61 m). I used two 15 footers (4.57 m) and one 16 footer (4.88 m). You start holding the ridgepole up by spiking a 2½ foot (0.76 m) post to the ridgepole on one end, and spike another post at the other end. Then, fill in a post above each beam in between the two posts already in place. Roof support logs lie on top of the ridge pole and extend across the plate log to about 1½ feet (0.46 m) past the wall logs. You will need seventy 3-4 inch (7.6-10.2 cm) diameter roof support logs, 10 feet (3.1 m) long each. You will need to cut their top ends at an angle where they meet the other roof support logs on top of the ridge pole. The larger diameter end of the log goes on top of the ridge pole. Try to keep all the logs the same diameter. You will need to fill in the gable ends (front and rear of the cabin) with logs. It will take about eleven 6½ footers (2 m), or you can use any leftover wall logs you might have. The lengths given for the logs are for vertical style logs but will work for a horizontal style cabin as well with some minor changes.

The add-on uses much fewer logs than the main cabin. This is partly because one whole side of the add-on is the main cabin itself. Also the add-on has only a 7 feet (2.1 m) high ceiling on the side where it joins the cabin, and it is 5½ feet (1.7 m) high on the other side. I made my add-on 8 by 28 feet (2.44 x 8.53 m). You can make it longer if you wish. For the add-on you will need 5 treated support piers of 8 inches (20.3 cm) diameter each; placed every 7 feet (2.13 m) apart for the sill logs to rest upon. Or you can use cement with rebar or cement blocks instead of treated lumber. You will need 5 sill logs, three at 10 feet (3.1 m) long and two at 8 feet (2.44 m) long. (Note that I used these lengths of sill and plate logs so that I could handle their weight while working alone). They should be 10 to 12 inches (25 to 30.5 cm) in diameter. You will need 22 joists each 8 feet (2.44 m) long and 5-6 inches (13-15 cm) in diameter and placed every 16 inches (40.6 cm) apart. You can make the wall logs to be either the horizontal or vertical style log lay out. The vertical wall logs (or post to fit horizontal logs to) should be about 4 feet 8 inches long (1.42 m). For an all vertical style building, just make them all 4 feet 8 inches long (1.42 m), the same as the upright posts. The exception to this is the two ends of the add-on which slope down from the main cabin where each will be a different length. You will need 2 plate logs 10 feet (3.1 m) long and one at 12 feet (3.66 m) long, each being 8-10 inches (20-25 cm) in diameter. Additionally, you will need two plate logs to go across each of the ends of the add-on at 9½ feet (2.9 m) long each. You will need 21 beam logs 9½ feet (2.9 m) long, 5-6 inches (13-15 cm) in diameter, and placed every 16 inches (40.6 cm) apart. These go from the main cabin across the plate log and extend out beyond the cabin wall to provide protection from the rain on the wall logs. While cutting down a tree and deciding what it would be used for I would use the base (which is larger in diameter) for either a sill or plate log at about 8 or 10 feet (2.44 or 3.1 m) in length (plus a couple of inches (5 cm) extra since it is a rough cut). Then, depending on the diameter of the remaining tree top, I could cut a wall log at eight feet (2.44 m) length or maybe instead a 12¼ foot (3.73 m) joist or beam, or instead a 10 foot (3.1 m) roof support log.

When deciding what to cut, keep in mind the diameter and lengths that you need for each type of log and for what it will be used for. Place the logs in stacks according to what they will be used for on the cabin. It is okay to have extra wall logs for the main cabin because they can easily be used on the add-on latter if not needed for the main cabin. It is best to complete to main cabin first before cutting logs for the add-on since you probably will have some left over wall logs that you can use.

6   GETTING STARTED

By now you should know the approximate number and length of all the logs you will need to cut. Keep a record each day of what you cut and what its planned use is to be so you can tell when you have all of the different size logs that are needed to build the cabin cut and ready to go. You will find that about two thirds of your time, about two months, will be spent cutting trees into logs of the proper size, peeling the bark off them, and then stacking them to dry near the location where you intend to build the cabin. As I went, I also cut up the part of the tree which I couldn't use for the cabin into firewood so it would be dryer for the coming winter.

There are some safety precautions to use when cutting down a tree. You should look the tree over to see which way it is leaning, and then cut it down so it will fall in the direction that it is leaning. Don't cut trees down on an overly windy day. Remember to have a pathway planned for you to move away from the tree once it starts to fall. If the falling tree lands on another standing tree as it falls, then it can kick back in the opposite direction several feet. So make sure you back away several feet after the tree starts to fall.

When you have decided which way you want the tree to fall, first make a horizontal cut straight into the tree about one third of the way through the tree on the side of the direction that you want the tree to fall. Second, make about a forty-five degree diagonal cut going up to meet up with the end of the horizontal cut. Third, make a horizontal cut on the opposite side slightly higher and cutting toward the previous cuts to within 1/10th of the tree's thickness. Start it about 2 inches (5 cm) above the other horizontal cut. If the tree doesn't fall, then you can drive a wedge into the last horizontal cut to help the tree to start falling. I could usually get the tree to start falling by pushing on it.

Next you will cut off the side limbs of the fallen tree. Then take a steel measuring tape and mark off the log at the length for which it will be used for the different type cabin logs. On a typical 12 inch (30.5 cm) diameter tree, you might get two 8-feet (2.44 m) long wall logs and one 10-feet (3.1 m) long roof support log or one 8-foot wall log and one 12 feet (3.66 m) long beam or joist. You can use a large crayon to mark off the place to be cut or use a pocket knife to cut out a triangle in the bark. You can use the cut out triangle area to hold the tape measure to start measuring for the second log length to be cut. Be sure to add 2 inches (5 cm) beyond the required amount so you can make a straighter more accurate cut when needed latter.

It is best not to build with the logs immediately, but to wait one year for the logs to dry after the bark is peeled due to the shrinkage in diameter that will occur. However, I didn't wait, and it didn't seem to make too much of a difference. I was amazed at how much the logs had dried out in two months' time evidenced by who much lighter the logs became. This was especially true for the spruce but not so much for the birch as it remained heavy. Next, clear the brush away from the area in which you intend to build the cabin. Then mark off the shape of the cabin with stakes. You can tie a string to the stakes if you want to (I did not). It is best to mark it off 2 feet (0.6 m) longer and wider than the actual size so you can build within the staked out boundary. I just used four sticks, one for each corner. If you decide to tie a string to your stakes, you do not have to string off the entire length of the cabin, but can set a stake to tie a string to at 6 feet (1.8 m) or so from your corner stake. Some use a compass to set the cabin lay out roughly. To check the corner for square measure from the 90 degree corner 6 feet (1.8288 m) and mark it. In the other direction measure 8 feet (2.4384 m) and mark it. If the corner is square, then a stick (or steel measuring tape) 10 feet (3.1 m) long will fit perfectly across the two marked points. You are now ready to start working on the foundation.

Stacking logs

Peeling bark off a birch tree with draw knife

7 FOUNDATION, SILL LOGS, AND JOISTS

After marking off your cabin's shape with stakes and a string if needed, you are ready to start the foundation. Again, I just placed one stake at each corner of where the cabin was to be placed, strings get in the way. There are several options for the foundation. For my main cabin, I laid two 8 by 8 inch (20.3 by 20.3 cm) by 4 feet (1.22 m) long pressure treated lumber pieces on top of gravel. This is called a piling type foundation. First, I dug out the top soil down to gravel in the shape of the treated lumber which I intended to lay down there. The top soil was thin there and was less than 1 foot (0.3 m) down to gravel. If it had been any more, I would have dug down one foot and filled the hole with gravel in the area I planned to lay the foundation log (pier or piling). The reason for using gravel instead of just placing the wood directly on top of the soil is because the gravel will drain water away. Well drained gravel is less likely to allow the wood to rot compared to damp dirt. Some people put a one to two foot thick gravel pad down right on top of the tundra (without removing any vegetation)

This works best for permafrost areas. The gravel pad would be about 14 by 42 feet (4.3 by 12.8 m) in this case. Then you would place the pier or piling on top of the gravel pad. Again, the gravel pad would be used for when building on permafrost type soil. After laying the two 8" x 8" x 4' (20.3 x 20.3 cm by 1.22 m) treated lumber pilings on top of each other, I then used a ½ inch (1.3 cm) drill bit and drilled through both 8 by 8 inch (20.3 by 20.3 cm) logs and then drove a ½ inch (1.3 cm) rebar rod through both pieces of lumber to hold them together. On the add-on part of the cabin, I dug out the top soil down to gravel and then put a 6 by 6 inch (15 by 15 cm) pier of the length I needed down into the hole in a vertical position. I would have used an 8 by 8 inch (20.3 by 20.3 cm) post if I had had it. I placed the 6 by 6 inch (15 by 15 cm) post on a footing of a 6 by 6 inch (15 by 15 cm) by 1 foot (0.31 m) post turned to the horizontal position and held together with two gusset plates, with one nailed on each side. Gusset plates are used to hold trusses together instead of nails. The 1 foot (0.31 m) long post turned to the horizontal position is called a footing. It helps to prevent the post from sinking into the ground under the load of the house. Along with the gusset plates, I recommend connecting the footing to the post with 12 to 18 inches (30.5 to 46 cm) of ½ inch (1.3 cm) rebar placed through the center. After all of your piers are in place, brace them together by crisscrossing two 2 by 4 inch (5 by 10.2 cm) boards between each pier. Instead of wood piers, some use cement blocks.

For permafrost ground (as I mentioned earlier) you can lay one foot of gravel down forming a pad directly over the undisturbed top soil and moss. You would then use pilings rather than piers for the foundation, like I did for the main cabin. On permafrost you will need to leave the crawl space under the cabin unskirted so air can flow through to prevent the ground from unthawing.

It is best to use pressure treated lumber for piers. I liked the ease of using the dimensional lumber 8 inch x 8 inch (20.3 x 20.3 cm) that I used. For other options a

25 foot (7.6 m) long telephone pole can be cut into the lengths needed. Some people even use untreated spruce, but never use birch or aspen where they would be touching the ground. It is recommended in conventional building practices that you dig the pier hole at least one foot deeper than the frost line. The frost line is the depth at which the soil freezes down to in the winter. In the interior of Alaska that is about 4 feet (1.22 m) down. If you are on gravel, which doesn't hold much water, I feel it's not necessary, but it is a judgment call you will have to make depending on the soil and conditions where you build. If you don't dig down a foot below the frost line, the cabin may frost heave, especially the first winter. However, it could be fine after that as the dirt dries out due to your cabin keeping the rain off. If needed, the house can be leveled by jacking up the sill log off of the pier and inserting blocks in between the pier and sill log (or the pier and the ground) to raise a side if needed.

Now back to the subject of the posts. They should be placed every 8 feet (2.44 m) apart so that your sill log ends meet on top of a post (piling or pier). The best way to lay the foundation on uneven ground is the way that I did the add-on, which was with vertical posts, but use 8 by 8 inch (20.3 by 20.3 cm) lumber. This way you can cut each off at the proper height to make the top level with all the other posts. Using pilings as I did on the main cabin is easier.

There are different ways for getting the piers all level. What I did was to start with one at the height I wanted so as to allow about two feet of crawl space under the house. So cut the first pier, which should be the pier located on the highest part of the ground on which your house will be built, at 1½ feet (0.46 m) above the ground. 1½ feet (0.46 m) plus your 12 inch (30.5 cm) sill log, minus 2 inches (5.1 cm) to flatten the sill log on top and bottom, minus 4 inches (10.2 cm) for the joist slot, equals about 2 feet (0.61) of crawl space. Anyway, from this first pier nail a string on the top and pull and hold the string over the location of where the next pier is to go. Place a small bubble level, which is made to hook onto a string, onto the middle of the string. Now raise or lower the string until the bubble is centered. This is the place where you will mark the next pier to cut off. If the ground is fairly level then you can just eye it or place a 2 x 4 inch (5 x 10 cm) board out to where the next pier will be to see if it looks to be on the same level. Finish cutting and placing all your piers. If you find that it is not level, you can jack it up and make small corrections if needed later by adding a block or cement brick as needed.

Next, you will need to cut half cut notches on your sill logs so they can fit together. I used a black crayon to mark off the cut. First, find the center of the log looking at its end, and mark a horizontal line across the end of the log. Then mark along the center, side of the log back one foot on both sides. I used a 90 degree square to help me mark it straight. Now join the two lines with a line across the top of the log. You are now ready to cut out the notch with the chain saw. There are some pictures at the end of chapter 11 (ADDING ON TO THE SIDE OF THE CABIN) of me doing this. With the log lying flat on the ground, hold the chain saw above the log and cut straight down toward the mark leaving about ¼ to ½ inch (0.6 to 1.3 cm) at the bottom, continue making these cuts toward the end of the log about every ½ inch (1.3 cm) apart. Next, take a sledge hammer and knock these out. Now turn the saw 45 degrees and make little cuts across the notch to make it smoother. Then turn it back the other direction and do the same thing. Next hold the saw perpendicular to the log again. Tilt the saw a little on its side and run the saw lightly across the log to smooth it out like you would a power belt sander. Cut another half cut notch on the other end, but on the opposite side. Next, flatten off the top and bottom of the log about ½ to ¾ inch (1.3 to 1.9 cm) deep on each side the full length of the log by running the chain saw across like a power sander again. After cutting all the sill logs with notches, fit them together on the ground in the way they are to be put up on the posts.

Actually, I pieced mine together beside the piers as I wanted to make sure I had the right length and fit on each log. Now start connecting the sill logs to the piers by placing the sill log up on the pier and then drilling a ½ inch (1.3 cm) hole about 15 inches (38 cm) deep through the sill log half cut notch's center and down into the pier. Drive ½ inch (1.3 cm) rebar through the hole connecting the sill log and the pier together with a sledge hammer. Next, put the next sill log half cut notch over this notch and drive two 6 to 8 inch (15.2 to 20.3 cm) spikes in on either side of the rebar. Continue connecting sill logs together until done. Next, use a chain saw as a power sander to flatten the tops of the sill logs where they overlap at the notch if any are not smooth.

You are now ready to start cutting out the mortise and tenon joint notches into the sill logs, one every 16 inches (40.6 cm) apart, for the joists to fit into. There are some pictures at the end of chapter 11 (ADDING ON TO THE SIDE OF THE CABIN) of me doing this. Start the first notch 16 inches (40.6 cm) over from the center of the end sill log. The cuts should be 4 inches back, 4 inches wide, and 4 inches down (10.2 by 10.2 by 10.2 cm). I used a square that has a level on one side to mark it. Place the square in a level position up against the sill log on the side you wish to cut the notch out. Mark off 4 inches back, 4 inches down, and 4 inches wide with a dark crayon (10.2 by 10.2 by 10.2 cm). Cut it out with the nose of the chain saw. Be careful. The chain saw sometimes grabs and jerks up. Cut several cuts within the 4 inch (10.2 cm) markings and then use a hammer to knock out the pieces. Then use the chain saw like a power sander to clean up the mortise and tenon joint.

Now all you have to do is cut the ends of the joists to fit into the mortise and tenon joint notches. Nail the joists into the notches with 6 inch (15 cm) long spikes. You will also need to flatten the top of the joist down about ½ inch (1.3 cm) using the chain saw as a power sander as mentioned before. This work with the foundation and sill logs goes kind of slow, but is important to be done right. Putting up the wall logs goes a lot faster.

Piers, sill logs and joist

8   FLOORING AND UP WITH THE WALL, PLATE LOGS AND BEAMS

Before putting up any wall logs, it is best to first prepare all the plate logs like you did the sill logs. The length of the plate logs depends on what style log cabin you intend to build: horizontal or vertical logs. If all your logs are to be vertical (stockade style), then the length does not matter. Cut the plate log length as long as you want as long as you can handle the weight and pick it up. If it is to be a horizontal style cabin, then the length of your wall logs will determine the location of the half cut notch in the plate log which should go on top of a vertical wall log. Your horizontal wall logs will be from 8 to 10 feet (2.44 to 3.1 m) long, whatever you can handle lifting up. So the vertical logs into which the horizontal logs will be nailed are to be placed every 8 to 10 feet (2.44 to 3.1 m) apart, with the half cut notch of the plate log being centered above a vertical log. If you use all vertical (stockade style) wall logs then you will not have to worry about the length of the plate log since its half cut notch will always end up on top of a vertical wall log.

The plate logs are joined together with half cut notches through the middle section of the house, and with saddle notches at the four corners of the cabin. A saddle notch is like a half cut notch (1 foot (0.3 m) or so length of log cut half way down the diameter of the log) but the saddle notch leaves 2 feet (0.61 m) of the whole log intact on the end past the half cut notch area. The two long 13 foot (3.96 m) end plate logs, across the front and back of the house, have regular half cut notches on each end with the top part of the notch being cut out. The four corner plate logs which connect to the two long 13 foot (3.96 m) end plate logs have the saddle notch cut out so that when fitted together two feet of the whole log extends past the cabin wall logs. These 2 feet (0.61 m) of log past the notch gives you the roof overhang to keep rain off the wall logs in the front and back of the cabin. So lay all of the plate logs out on the ground to make sure they fit.

Also, before starting with the wall logs, you might want to lay down your plywood floor. If you wait until after putting up the wall logs, then you will have to cut out the edges of the plywood where the plywood butts up against the wall logs. You can then stuff fiberglass insulation into any gap between the plywood and wall log. That is what I did on the main cabin and it wasn't too much trouble. This kept my plywood floor out of the rain and allowed my wall logs to sit directly on top of the sill logs instead of sitting on plywood. The disadvantage is that it is harder to put up the wall logs while standing on top of the round joist logs. I laid a loose piece of plywood down on top of the joist to stand on as I worked. I put the plywood down on top of the joist first on the add-on before putting up the wall logs.

Flatten off about the top ½ inch (1.3 cm) of the joist. Don't cut off too much. I slid a 2 by 4 inch (5.1 by 10.2 cm) by 8 feet (2.44 m) board across the top and cut down the high spots. If your joists don't end up level enough after this, then you will have to lay 1 by 4 inch (2.54 by 10.2 cm) boards every 1 foot (0.3 m) apart across the entire length of the cabin floor. The 1 x 4s (2.54 by 10.2 cm) boards each need to start and end on top of a joist. Next, lay the ¾ inch (1.9 cm) tongue and groove plywood down. The ends should start and end on top of a joist. Drive an 8d nail or 1¾ inch (4.44 cm) deck screw into the tongue at a 45 degree angle every 6 inches (15 cm). This floor should work if your joist are firm enough, but if it appears to be weak and have too much give in it as you walk across it, you can add another layer of plywood on top where the edges do not end up on top of the first layer of plywood. To do this, start by using a cut in half (4 feet by 4 feet) (1.22 by 1.22 m) piece of plywood. This way the length edges of the plywood will not be on top of the first layer. Note that you can put the plywood in after completing the cabin shell (walls and roof) if you choose. The advantage is that the wall logs sit directly on top of the sill logs and your plywood stays dry.

You are now ready to start putting up wall logs. You start out with the two corner wall logs and two other wall logs. You should use some nice 10-12 inch (25-30.5 cm) diameter logs at the corners. Cut these logs to 8 foot (2.44 m) lengths exactly. Flatten the sides a little where the other logs will fit up to them, especially if the log is not straight or has a knot or bulge of some type. With one nail each, nail two 2 by 4 inch by 8 foot (5 by 10 cm by 2.44 m) boards 90 degrees apart onto the top sides of each of the four 8 foot (2.44 m) long wall logs. I nailed mine at about 5 feet (1.5 m) up. These are temporary boards used to hold the wall log up until the plate & other wall logs & beam logs are in place. Now stand one of the corner logs up and level it so that it isn't leaning in any direction. It helps to have someone stand back a little and tell you when it looks straight. Then, while you hold it in place straight, have them drive the other nail in the 2 by 4 inch (5 by 10 cm) board into the sill log. Without a helper, you just have to try to hold the corner wall log up by the 2 x 4 (5 x 10 cm) board as you work your way down and nail the other end of the 2 x 4 inch (5x10 cm) board into the sill log. To stand the corner wall log up square I just used my eye to get them straight, but if you have trouble, you can use a string bob. Just let the string bob hang off the sides all the way around the log. If the log isn't straight up and down, then the string bob will lean away from the log in the direction the log is leaning. Stand back twenty feet or so away from the log from different sides to see if it looks straight. Drive an 8 inch (20 cm) spike 45 degrees (toe nailed) on the inside of the cabin connecting the wall log to the sill log. In order to prevent the bottom of the wall log from sliding off the center of the sill log as you toe nail the 8 inch (20 cm) spike, you can temporarily place a 5 inch (13 cm) mini spike at the base of the wall log on the opposite side into the sill log. This prevents the wall log from moving as you toe nail it to the sill log. Do the other corner log the same way. The location of the other two wall logs depends, as I wrote earlier in this chapter, on the length of plate logs used and should be placed so that the half notch of the plate log sits on top of the wall log. Next, put the 13 feet (3.96 m) long, end plate log up on top of the two vertical corner logs, and nail it in place with one 8 inch (20 cm) spike into the half notch at each end. To get the plate log up there, I raised and placed one end on top of a corner wall log, and, while still holding the other end, I climbed a ladder and placed it on top of the other vertical corner wall log. Make sure no one is below it because it can be tricky to get one side to stay while you raise the other one. If there are two of you, then both could lift up on one end at the same time or at least hold one in place on top of the corner wall log while you raise the other end. Next place another wall log cut to exactly eight feet length on the sill log in the location where the plate log's half notch cut will rest on top of the wall log. As before, use two temporary 2 x 4 inch (5 x 10 cm) boards to hold the wall log up straight. Level and toe nail as before. Now you are ready to place up two more plate logs going to the other two vertical wall logs from the corner wall logs. Leave the temporary 2 by 4 inch by 8 foot 5 x 10 cm x 2.44 m) lumber in place until you finish this section. Next, frame in your door and plan the location of your windows. (See chapter 9 Doors and Windows.)

You may now start filling in the wall logs. Work starts to go a lot faster from here on. For both vertical as well as horizontal style logs, you will need to cut a little off the sides with the chain saw to get as close of a fit as possible. The closer the fit, the less chinking will be necessary; also the house will be warmer. The way I did it was to place the next wall log to be fitted in place next to the log that is in place. Then I could see and mark with a crayon any high places on the log that stood out and prevented a close fit. Then place the log on the ground and cut off these high places with the chain saw using it like a power sander as explained before. Cut some off the opposite side as well to get it good and straight for the next log that will be standing up to it. Now check it out again and cut more off if necessary or nail it in place if it looks okay. Don't forget to alternate the ends of the wall logs so that the bigger diameter end of one connects up to the smaller end of the next wall log that goes up, back and forth. After getting a good fit between two wall logs, place a piece of sill seal fiberglass insulation in between the two logs. Sill seal is a fiberglass insulation which comes in long rolls which are 1 inch (2.5 cm) thick and 4 inches (10 cm) wide and comes in colors of yellow and pink. Yellow is the best choice for looks. It is important to use four-inch wide (10cm) fiberglass sill seal that has been folded in half, in between the logs as you put them up. You will be spreading Perma-Chink over this fiberglass (inside and out of the cabin). Perma-Chink is a type of caulk that comes in a 5 gallon (19 liter) bucket and is used to seal between the cracks or joints where the logs meet. More about Perma-Chink later in this chapter.

For fitting together vertical logs, simply place the newly fitted wall log about one inch away from the last wall log nailed in. Lightly start to drive in the top spike, going down through the plate log into the wall log, to hold it in place with about one inch of space between wall logs. Before driving in the spike through the plate log, using a half inch drill, drill about 2-3 inches (5-7.6 cm) down into the plate log. Use a 4 inch long bolt to finish driving in the spike after it enters the ½ inch (1.3 cm) hole. The reason for drilling the hole and not just using a longer spike is due to the possibility of the plate log splitting since a spike is driven down every 8 inches (20 cm) or so. With a screw driver or putty knife, force the sill seal in between the two logs. The sill seal should be folded in half. Next, hit the top of the vertical wall log to knock it over against the other wall log. It won't move if you drove the plate log spike too far down into the wall log. While holding the vertical wall log as tight as possible against the other wall log, finish nailing the top spike down into the wall log with the 6 or 8 inch (15 or 20 cm) spike. I did this by myself using my left arm to hold them together and my right arm to drive the spike in enough to hold it in place. Then toe nail the bottom of the wall log into the sill log as before.

For horizontal style logs, first tilt the log up a little and poke the fiberglass sill seal in. Toe nail both ends of the horizontal wall log into the two vertical wall logs. Where the two wall logs meet at the 90 degree corner the vertical log there uses what is called a corner-post type notch. The corner-post notch has two sides flattened to have the wall logs but up to and toe nailed into it.

After filling in these three sides with wall logs, you will put in the beams next before doing the next section of wall logs. The beams are done the same way as the joist except that I used 3 inch wide by 3 inch down by 3 inch back (7.6 x 7.6 x 7.6 cm) cuts for the mortise and tenon notch. If your plate logs are 12 inches (30 cm) in diameter then you can make a 4 inch (10 cm) mortise and tenon notch. Place one notch every 16 inches (41 cm) apart. About every five beams, recheck the overall distance from the starting point to make sure both sides of the beams are the same distance away from the starting point. You are now ready to go to the next section of plate logs, wall logs, and beams starting with a wall log held in place by two temporary 2 x 4 inch (5 x 10 cm) boards as before. I prefer the vertical log style rather than the horizontal piece-en-piece. Another option for wall logs instead of vertical (stockade) or horizontal piece-en-piece is, if your logs are of similar diameter, to not use a vertical log to join the horizontal logs to every 8 to 10 feet (2.44 to 3.1 m) (depending on the length of your wall logs). You can use a half lap notch to continue the horizontal style to the end corner post (the length of the cabin) as long as you place each half lap notch on top of a solid log and spike it with staggered spikes about every 3 feet (1 m) and using two spikes in the half lap notch. You will need to put in the beams every 10 feet (3 m) or so as you go along before finishing the wall to the end to keep the wall from leaning in or out. I like the vertical (stockade) style best of the three types and feel that it is a stronger wall.

In the vertical style log cabin, as the logs dry out, they sometimes get a crack that opens up in the log. If a log gets a split or crack in it at its base by the floor, cold air can get in. Use a screw driver and poke some fiberglass into the crack or caulk up the hole to prevent air from flowing through the crack from beneath the floor.

The following should be done after putting on the roof, but since it concerns the wall logs I choose to write about it here. You will need to put Perma-Chink in between your logs on top of the fiberglass sill seal. Perma-Chink is a type of caulk which looks like mud or cement chink like they used in the old days. In the real old days people used moss instead of fiberglass and clay or mud to cover it. Perma-Chink comes in several different colors or shades to choose from. It is more flexible than caulk and expands and contracts well in summer and winter temperatures. It comes in 5 gallon (19 liter) buckets as well as in regular caulk tubes. The caulk tubes cost more to use. Perma-Chink doesn't stick to mildew. Use bleach to remove any mildew first. Then rinse and let dry before applying the Perma-Chink. Also, Perma-Chink does not go on to green logs very well. It is best to wait one year for the logs to dry before applying Perma-Chink. The sill seal fiberglass insulation kept our house's heat in fine our first winter without the Perma-Chink even though noise passed easily through the fiberglass. To apply, start out by placing a special canvas bag into a six inch diameter piece of chimney pipe. The special canvas bag is a heavy duty bag similar to the type bakers use to decorate cakes. It is sold where they sell the Perma-Chink. You can scoop in the Perma-Chink with a putty knife into the bag. Squeeze the bag and force the Perma-Chink out onto the sill seal fiberglass insulation and into the crack in between the logs. After emptying the bag of Perma-Chink, place the bag in a bucket of water to keep it from drying out or place it in the bucket that the Perma-Chink came in and close the lid. Next, with a spray gun, spray a mist of water over the Perma-Chink. Then use a thin putty knife to smooth out the Perma-Chink and make sure it touches the logs on both sides. It should be about ¼ inch (6 mm) thick when you are finished spreading it. The Perma-Chink sales a backer foam strip to place between the logs for the Perma-Chink to be spread on. It works well also, but I preferred the fiberglass.

You will need steps to get up into the house. Installing the steps now will make it easier to enter the cabin as you complete all the other tasks that need to be done. Lumber yards sell pre-cut out steps. Simply trim them down for the height needed.

Then nail 2 by 6 inch (5 by 15 cm) boards across the top of them. I also nailed a 2 by 6 inch (5 by 15 cm) board across the back with which I nailed onto the sill log below the door.

Skirting around the open areas below the sill logs makes the cabin look better and also keeps animals out and, if insulated, the cold out. Skirting should be done after the house is completed. There is a case for when you should not use skirting. If you build on top of permafrost ground that is made up of anything other than gravel, then you will not be able to skirt the house. This is because you don't want any heat from your house to melt the permafrost soil underneath and thus cause your house to sink into the ground. Two feet wide rolls of aluminum roof flashing works well for skirting. You can use either galvanized steel or aluminum skirting. It should be pointed out that fire insurance companies usually require the house to be skirted in order to get coverage. Leave two openings where the skirting can be pulled back enough so that you can crawl under the house. Where the skirting crosses over this access area, you need to use a nail and punch several holes in it for ventilation during the summertime. You will insulate around the skirting next. I used 1½ inch (38 mm) bead board rigid insulation at first, but it wasn't good enough. Next, I added some R-19 fiberglass insulation. To do this, first crawl under the house with some chicken wire and nail it onto the sill log all the way around except at the two entry ways. Next, unroll the fiberglass and place it underneath the wire. The chicken wire should hold it in place. It will prove easier to place the insulation in before the chicken wire, provided it will stay up in place. For the entry doors you can glue some fiberglass onto a piece of plywood that covers the hole.

Below the floor itself some fiberglass insulation will be needed. Use at least R-19 insulation. Use chicken wire again to hold the fiberglass in place up under the floor. Insulation should also be placed in the cubby holes in between the roof support logs. Simply fill the hole up with fiberglass insulation. Complete both of these tasks after completing the cabin or at least the roof is on.

Up with the wall and plate logs

Up with the wall and plate logs and beams

Putting Perma-Chink into applier bag

Applying Perma-Chink in between logs

Using a putty knife and water spray to spread Perma-Chink

9 DOORS AMD WINDOWS

You can make your own doors and windows or buy them already made and just install them. The roof should be on before installing the actual windows, but it is good to put the rough frame that the window and door is to fit into as you go along building the walls. It is much cheaper to build your own, especially the windows. If the door frame is not square, then you will have to either fix it or else make your door to match. I made the frame out of 2 by 6 inch (5 by 15 cm) boards 77 inches (196 cm) high by 33½ inches (85 cm) wide. This is as far as you go with the frame until you hang the door. The door is 33 inches (84 cm) wide by 76½ inches (194 cm) high. The door itself is just six 2 by 6 inch 5 by 15 cm) boards laid side by side. They are held together with a horizontal 2 by 6 inch (5 by 15 cm) board located at the top and bottom of the door and with one diagonal 2 by 6 inch (5 by 15 cm) board going across in between the two horizontal boards. Don't put the top and bottom horizontal boards all the way to the ends of the vertical boards. They should be about 4 inches (10 cm) from the ends. Place either some fiberglass or caulk or both in between the boards. Also, be sure to get the vertical boards as tight as you can get them while nailing the horizontal boards to them. Simply place two nails into the horizontal board above where each of the vertical boards lay beneath it. The diagonal board needs only one nail going into each vertical board. Hang the door with three hinges. You should use a chisel to cut out an area as wide and deep as the hinge is into the frame so it will be recessed and flush. You don't have to bother recessing the hinge into the door itself. After hanging the door, install the doorknob. You will need a doorknob hole cutter. It is meant to be used with an electric drill, but I didn't have electricity back then, so I used my hand drill to turn it. I used the hand drill to drill a 1 inch (2.5 cm) hole into the wall as well for where the locking parts of the door knob parts go. After installing the doorknob, you are now ready to install the door jam and seal. I used 1 by 2 ($^3/_4$ by 1½ actual size) inch (2.5 by 5 cm) furring boards. But first nail or stick the insulation you intend to use onto the furring which has been cut to length. The stores have several types of strip insulation for doors to choose from. To install the furring, with the door in the shut position, place the furling up against the door and nail four or five nails through the furring into the door frame. Now caulk all the cracks in between where the 2 by 6 inch (5 by 15 cm) board door frame and the furring meet and over all the nails with a good quality caulk.

There are two basic ways to build and install your own windows. Windows that do not open to let fresh air in or to allow you a way of escape out in case of fire are the easiest to make. First make a rough frame for the finished window to be inserted into. To make the rough frame for the window to be inserted into just nail two 3 inch (7.6 cm) nails into each end of a 2 x 6 inch (5 by 15 cm) board to form a rough frame about ½ inch (1.3 cm) wider and taller than the finished window that is to be installed into it. The horizontal top board of this frame should cover the full length of the frame having the vertical boards located underneath it. Flatten the logs of the cabin a little where this rough frame of the 2 x 6 inch (5 by 15 cm) boards is to connect to the cabin for a better fit. Before nailing the rough frame to the log of the cabin add a strip of sill seal fiberglass insulation. This rough frame of 2 x 6 inch (5 by 15 cm) boards, if cut squarely, usually nails up square without any help needed and you can use a square to check its shape for squareness. Connect the rough frame to the cabin logs by driving two 4 - 5 inch (10 - 13 cm) nails into each of the four sides. Remember to flatten the logs a little where the rough frame of 2 x 6 inch (5 x 15 cm) boards connect for a better fit. It is best to leave it like this until the roof is on. This is your rough frame and it is ready for either a store bought window or a homemade window to be inserted into its space.

To finish it using store bought windows, simply slide the window into the rough 2 x 6 inch (5 x 15 cm) frame inserting fiberglass around the window and nail the finished window to the frame. To finish it using homemade windows that can't be opened up: use some 1½ inch (3.8 cm) long finish nails, and nail on four 1 by 2 inch (2.5 by 5 cm) furring boards (one on each 2 x 6 inch (5 x 15 cm) rough frame boards). Nail the furring ¼ of an inch (6 mm) from the edge of the 2 by 6 inch (5 by 15 cm) board. Next, using a clear silicone caulk, caulk around the inside bottom edge of the furring. Place the first pane of glass in place before the caulk dries. Caulk lightly along the glass. The glass should be about ¼ of an inch (6 mm) smaller than the frame it is inserted into. Add four more 1 by 2 inch (1.3 by 5 cm) furrings next to the glass and nail in place to the 2 x 6 inch (5 by 15 cm) boards using finish nails. Drive the finish nails down under the wood so that it is not visible with a finish nail driver. Caulk around the edge of the furring again as well as over the nail heads. Place in the second window pane (and caulk) and then add the final furring to hold it in place. To finish up, caulk around the wood furring next to the glass and over the nail heads inside and out. You can place 1 by 4 inch (2.5 by 10 cm) boards over the gap where the window board meets up to the wall log for a nice looking finish on the inside and out. On the outside add a strip of aluminum about 4 inches (10 cm) wide in between the bottom of the log that goes across the top of the window and the window frame to help insure that rain does not get in.

To make homemade windows that open up is similar. It is best to put the window together on a dry day. The easiest way is to make a square frame out of 2 by 4 inch (5 by 10 cm) boards ¼ of an inch (6 mm) larger than the window glass is to be. It is best to use screws instead of nails for this window is to be opened and shut as needed. Next, place four ½ inch (1.3 cm) wide wood trim pieces ¼ inch (6 mm) from the edge of the 2 by 4 inch (5 by 10 cm) board. Caulk with clear silicone as before. Place in your glass. Next, nail in four more 1 by 2 inch (2.5 by 5 cm) furrings. Caulk as before. Add your second window glass. Caulk again as before. Place in four more ½ inch (1.3 cm) wide trim pieces. Finish up with caulking around the wood trim pieces next to the window and the 2 by 4 inch (5 by 10 cm) board. Next build a rough frame out of 2 by 6 inch (5 by 15 cm) boards as described for the solid window before for this window to fit into. It should be ½ inch (1.3 cm) taller and wider than the 2 by 4 inch (5 by 10 cm) window frame you just made. Buy two hinges from the hardware store and recess them with a chisel to be flush in the 2 by 6 inch (5 by 15 cm) board frame. Connect the window assembly to the hinges making sure it is centered so as to open and shut freely. Next, nail in four 1 by 1 inch (2.5 by 2.5 cm) furring boards to act as a jam for where you want the window to stop sort of like was done on the door. You may have to use a drawknife or a pocket knife to round the edges of the window assembly so it will close properly without hitting on the one edge. To seal out air around the window when it is closed you can tape on a strip of ½ inch (1.3

cm) wide foam seal. It comes with the foam already attached to the tape. Use a simple hook latch to lock the window.

Rough frame for window insert

Homemade double pane window for back of add-on (I made this window to be used to open and shut. I used 2 x 6 inch (5 x 15 cm) boards but wished I had used 2 x 4 inch (5 x 10 cm) boards since it would open and shut easier. This size is best for non-opening window installations)

Homemade double pane window for back of add-on & similar to one used for kitchen window of the main cabin.

10   THE ROOF

You are now ready to do the roof. Start by preparing the ridge poles to be joined together by cutting half cut notches on the ends to be joined in a similar way as you did the plate logs. Carry the three ridgepoles up and lay them on top of the beams. Next carry up two of the 2½ feet (0.76 m) long logs which will hold the ridgepole up above the beams. These two should be cut to exactly 2½ feet (0.76 m) long (if you want a roof slope and pitch of an angle like my cabin). The ridgepole support log will be toe nailed with two 5 inch (13 cm) long spikes into the top of the beam at the location where the ends of the ridgepoles will meet and above the plate log on the end of the cabin. Remember that, on the two outside ends of the cabin, the ridgepole will extend 2 feet (0.61 m) past the outside edge of the ridgepole support log thus extending 2 feet (0.61 m) beyond the wall of the cabin. Next, place the ridgepole up on top of the two logs. On the outside end, which doesn't have the half lap notch in it, drill down one inch with the ½ inch (1.3 cm) drill bit at the location above the 2½ foot (0.76 m) support log. Drive a 6 inch (15 cm) long spike (depending on the diameter of the ridgepole) through the ridgepole and into the center of the 2½ foot (0.76 m) support log. Next, measure and cut to length each 2½ feet (0.76 m) long support log to go above each beam and secure as before. After finishing the first ridgepole with its 2½ feet (0.76 m) long support logs, move on to the next two ridgepoles logs and install in like manner. Next, you will be placing the 10 foot (3.1 m) long roof support logs across from the ridgepole down to and across the plate log. The large end of the 10 foot (3.1 m) long roof support log goes on top of the ridgepole, and its end should be cut at an angle so as to meet up flush with the other 10 feet (3.1 m) long roof log on the other side of the ridgepole. If there is any difference in the diameters of these logs, you will need to place them in order across the roof from largest to smallest. Drive a 6 inch (15 cm) long spike (depending on the diameter of the log itself) through the roof support log and into the ridgepole. On the other end, drive a 5 inch (13 cm) spike through the roof support log and into the plate log. Next, nail 2 by 4 inch (5 by 10 cm) boards flat on to the plate logs in between the roof support logs. These will be used to nail 1 by 4 inch (2.5 by 10 cm) boards onto to close off the gap between the plate log and roof. Don't forget to place two 10 foot (3.1 m) long roof support logs on each end of the cabin for the roof overhang where the ridgepole and plate logs extend two feet beyond the cabin.

Next, you will probably need to place three or four rows of 1 by 4 inch (2.5 by 10 cm) boards on each side of the ridgepole running the length of the cabin. Place the first row of 1 by 4 inch (2.5 by 10 cm) boards on both sides of the top of the ridgepole across the roof support logs. The 1 by 4 inch (2.5 by 10 cm) board end should start and end on top of a support log. Place the second row of 1 by 4 inch (2.5 by 10 cm) boards above the plate logs. Then place the third and fourth rows of 1 by 4 inch (2.5 by 10 cm) boards in between these two rows. Be sure to extend the

1 by 4 inch (2.5 by 10 cm) boards all the way across to the end of the roof overhang area as well. I didn't at first and that is why my roof slanted down on both ends until I fixed it.

Next, nail ½ inch (1.3 cm) plywood sheets across the top of the 1 by 4 inch (2.5 by 10 cm) boards. Try to drive the nails through both the 1 by 4 inch (2.5 by 10 cm) boards and the roof support logs. It is best to use tongue and groove plywood roof decking but it is not necessary. Caulk the cracks in between the plywood sheets. Place a roll of 10 mill plastic sheeting over the top of the plywood next. This needs to be done on a day that is not windy. Plastic can be very slippery to walk on, so start at one end and walk on top of the plywood while you unroll it across.

Next, you will lay down the bead board solid type insulation. Bead board comes in several thicknesses from 1 to 4 inches (2.5 to 10 cm) or more. The blue foam type is good with a higher R-value, but it costs more. Regular white Styrofoam bead board of 3 inch (7.6 cm) thickness will work okay. The thicker it is, the higher the R-value and betters the fuel savings. The white Styrofoam type has an R-value of 4.76 per inch of thickness depending on the density of Styrofoam that you use. I was on a tight budget and only used 1½ inches (3.8 cm) at first. The cabin held its heat okay at best and the snow on the roof would melt and form ice sheets when the temperature was not very cold outside. I ended up replacing it with R-Max. In order to save heating fuel, I took the plain Styrofoam off the main cabin and moved it to the add-on and doubled it giving three inches on the add-on. On the main cabin roof I then installed two 1½ inch 4' by 8' (3.8 cm 1.22 by 2.44 m) boards of R-Max insulation. R-Max is better than plain Styrofoam and has aluminum foil on both sides. I now had an R-value of 20 on the main cabin and 14 on the add-on. More insulation would have been better, but money was tight and to be honest, I was looking forward to having a boat with a jet type engine to go up the Salcha River fishing and exploring with. I did add a radiant barrier, which has open celled bubble wrap sandwiched between two layers of foil, to the inside ceiling of the house. I stapled it to the plywood. It was worth doing to retain radiant heat and made the ceiling look better as well.

To install the solid board insulation, lay two sheets of it starting at one end. On top of the bead board nail on a 1 by 4 inch (2.5 by 10 cm) by 8 or 12 feet (2.44 or 3.66 m) long board running parallel with the length of the house. It should be nailed close to the bottom. The tin roof will be fastened down onto these 1 by 4 inch (2.5 by 10 cm) boards. After nailing on the first 1 by 4 inch (2.5 by 10 cm) board at the bottom, nail three in the middle and one about five inches (13 cm) down from the top. Make sure to put the insulation all the way up to the top so it will meet with the other side when it is put on. Continue adding bead board and 1 by 4 inch (2.5 by 10 cm) boards across the rest of the roof as you stand on the bead board that is already nailed down.

For another option other than bead board you can use fiberglass insulation with a cold roof type construction. Fiberglass is less expensive when compared with bead board, but you will need to use several 2 by 8 inch (5 by 20 cm) boards placed every 24 inches (0.61 m) apart. This work also requires a little more carpenter skills to complete. The advantage of solid insulation board with a hot roof system over fiberglass, other than being easier to build and install, is that if fiberglass gets wet it will lose its insulating ability. But bead board retains its full R-value when wet and you do not have to vent an attic area.

Next, place the tin on the roof. You can buy tin that is 2 by 10 feet (0.61 by 3.1 m) or 3 by 10 feet (0.91 by 3.1 m). The 3 feet wide (0.91 m) tin will save you a little money, but it is heavier to work with. Use tin roof screws to hold the tin down.

The screws come in several lengths; I used 1 inch (2.5 cm). The screws have a rubber washer under the head which seals rain water out of the hole. The heads will take a small socket wrench and can be easily screwed in after first making a small hole in the tin. To make a hole you can either use a hammer to tap the screw itself into the tin or use a nail to punch the hole. Make sure the screws go into the 1 by 4 inch (2.5 by 10 cm) board beneath. Next, spray some of that foam type insulation in the crack across the top of the roof. Place the tin cap across the roof top next with the special tin cap that is made for such.

Outside view of roof support logs

Inside view of roof support logs

Rigid insulation

Working with rigid insulation

11   ADDING ON TO SIDE OF CABIN

Our second year I added on an 8 by 28 foot (2.44 by 8.53 m) section to the side of our cabin. It is best to plan for the add-on while building the cabin itself even if you put off building it. Planning ahead will prevent your windows from being cut off or made of no effect by the add-on. If you should so desire, you can build an 8 by 38 foot (2.44 by 11.58 m) add-on to both sides of your cabin, but this would block all of the side windows of the main cabin. Building the add-on section is similar to the building of the cabin itself. On the side of the add-on, which is 8 feet (2.44 m) away from the house, you will need to place a pier at each corner and every 8 feet (2.44 m) in between. But before doing the piers on that side of the add-on, you will need to prepare the main cabin to be connected onto. To do this, simply drive 6 inch (15 cm) spikes through 2 by 6 inch (5 by 15 cm) boards into the sill logs along the area of the cabin in which you wish to add on. Use a level to keep them straight. It is best to pre-drill ¼ inch (6 mm) holes through the 2 by 6 inch (5 by 15 cm) boards to prevent them from cracking when the spike goes through. The spikes should be spaced about every 2 feet (0.61 m) apart, but at least 6 inches (15 cm) away from the 2 by 6 inch (5 by 15 cm) boards' ends. Next, using 8 inch (20 cm) spikes, nail down a second layer of 2 by 6 inch (5 by 15 cm) boards across the ones just nailed down. Make sure you stagger the spikes so that they don't land on the other spikes. Into the cabin's wall logs you will be toe nailing joists that sit on top of these 2 by 6 inch (5 by 15 cm) boards. You may prepare your joist now if you like. The joist should be at least 5 inches (13 cm) in diameter. You will need to first flatten off a straight flat area across the top of the joist. Next, cut each end's underside down until you have 4 inches (10 cm) thickness from the top of the joist down. The end of the joist which will be going into the sill log with a mortise and tenon type joint should also have its sides cut down to 4 inches (10 cm) width. Prepare the sill logs of the add-on next. You will not need to add any sill logs next to the cabin because you are using the main cabin's own sill logs and piers to support one side of your add-on. Use half cut notches for your sill logs as you did on the main cabin. Next, determine the proper height for your piers so that the floor will be level. To do this you must take into account the diameter of your sill logs as you will soon see. Nail a string onto the top of the 2 by 6 inch (5 by 15 cm) boards on which the joists will rest. After placing a bubble level on the string, pull the string tight up against a yard stick that is placed in the hole for the pier. Note how many inches (cm) the string comes up to on the measuring stick while the bubble is in the level position. This measurement is the height to which the bottom of the joist will come to. To figure out the proper height for the pier itself, you must add 4 inches (10 cm), which is the height of the mortise and tenon notch, and then subtract the diameter of the sill log. This will give you the proper height for this pier. All of the piers will need to be done this same way since they may not be buried the same depth. If the ground is fairly level you can probably get by with just eyeing it to get the proper length for each pier. Place the proper height piers in each hole. Connect the sill logs to each other and the piers using rebar and spikes as you did for the main cabin. Next, cut the notches in the sill logs for the joist to fit into. Space them every 16 inches (40 cm) apart and spike both ends of the joist with a 6 inch (15 cm) spike. Add the plywood floor in the same way as was done for the main cabin. Onto the main cabin's wall logs, spike on one roll of 2 by 6 inch (5 by 15 cm) boards to support the beams as was done before to support the joist against the cabin. Extend these 2 x 6 inch (5 by 15 cm) boards 2 feet (0.61 m) beyond the cabin's length on both ends for a roof overhang. For the second roll of boards across the 2 by 6 inch (5 by 15 cm) boards, you will need to use 2 by 4 inch (5 by 10 cm) boards instead of the 2 by 6 inch (5 by 15 cm) boards which were used for the floor. The 2 by 4 inch (5 by 10 cm) boards will be lowered slightly in accordance with the slope of the beams and your roof. You will want to place these boards as high as possible so that you will have more head room inside the add-on. I placed the tops of my 2 by 6 inch (5 by 15 cm) boards at 80 inches (203.2 cm) above the plywood floor. Make sure you leave enough room to work. You have the beam at 4 to 5 inches (10 to 13 cm), a layer of 1 by 4 inch (2.5 by 10 cm) boards at 1 inch (2.5 cm) thickness, a layer of ½ inch (1.3 cm) plywood, 4 inches (10 cm) or more layer of bead board ridged insulation, another layer of 1 by 4 inch (2.5 by 10 cm) boards, and the bent tin roofing at 1 inch (2.5 cm). This all totals about 12 inches (30 cm). Make the other side of the add-on as high as possible too, but low enough to give the roof enough of a slope to allow the water to drain off. Continue to build the add-on as you did the main cabin: beams from the main cabin to the add-on wall, plywood, insulation, 1 x 4 inch (2.5 by 10 cm) boards for the tin to screw into, and the tin roof. Since the 4 by 8 foot (1.22 by 2.44 m) plywood on the roof will be a little short, nail on a 1 by 6 inch (5 by 15 cm) board to finish it out. Since the ridged insulation sheets come in 4 by 8 foot (1.22 by 2.44 m) lengths, you will also need to add the same amount of insulation over this gap or use fiberglass at the place where the add-on joins to the main cabin. You can use spray foam to insulate this small strip as well. Also, fill in the space in between the beams on top of the wall logs with fiberglass insulation.

Making the half cut notches

Making the half cut notches

Making the half cut notches

Making the half cut notches (Note the 2 x 6 inch (5 x 15 cm) board naided to the main cabin to suport the add-on joist)

Cutting mortise and tenon joints for joist

Joists in

Close up

Building the add-on (I was using left over logs from building the main cabin and they did not have the length I would have preferred for the roof overhang area)

Building the add-on

Close up

Back of add-on with homemade window on hinges that can open. I was working with logs that I had left over from building the main cabin and so they are not as uniform in length as I would have liked. Notice that I added a tin over hang to the back of the main cabin to keep snow and rain off stuff.

12 WELL WATER

I started by getting my drinking water from the river. But for about two months a year the river is dirty during and after spring break up. You can have someone drill you a well, but that would cost $3000 or more depending on the depth and what they drill through. What I did was drive a well point down using a jackhammer. This works in sand or gravel or dirt type soils. So if bedrock (sandstone, limestone type rock) is shallow or there are large rocks then you cannot drive a well. You can expect to drive the well point about 30 feet (9 m) at best. I first tried to drive the piping down using a sledge hammer. I got it about 6 feet (1.8 m) down with a lot of trouble and ended up with a messed up, bulged out pipe where I hit it. So I had to wiggle up and down on the pipe until I retrieved the well point. I then rented a jack hammer with a special attachment to drive the well point down. The key to success is to use two good sized pipe wrenches to tighten each joint more after every minute or less of jack hammer use. Having someone tightening as you use the jack hammer is even better and is what I did in this case. Be sure also to use Teflon tape around the pipe threads. I could get my pipe down only 20 feet (6 m), but with the river so near, and the water table so high, we always have water. I have been told that the well should go down at least 30 feet (9 m) to avoid getting surface water that might be contaminated. Check the regulations and suggestions given for your area. You should get the water tested before drinking it due to the possibility of arsenic and other minerals being in the ground. Alaska's water is not very good due to too much iron and other things in it. Water probably won't come out at first after driving the well point down. You need to pour some water down the well pipe until it fills up to the top. If the water in the pipe doesn't go back down the pipe or it goes down slowly, then you will need to open up the well point. To do this, you can wrap some electrical or duct tape around a broom or mop handle in one spot about 1 foot (0.3 m) from the end of the handle until it is just big enough to fit into the well pipe. Then force the mop handle with the tape seal on it down the well as hard as you can. Water will squirt up and around the tape, so have a towel and mop ready. Keep doing this as hard as you can until the water goes down on its own. What this does is to clear the dirt out away from the well point and its holes. If after thirty minutes the water still won't go down, then you may have to rent a high pressure water pump to force water down the well. I know a man who used dynamite to open his well up. After you open it up, then you are ready to hook up a pump. We put a simple hand pump on at first. Remember to locate the sewer leach field at least 100 feet (30 m) from the well. I added a long plastic pipe down the well. It just fit into the metal pipe of the well. This works better than just the metal piping that I drove down. If any of the metal piping's joint connections are not perfect and slowly leak; this plastic pipe fixes that problem.

Since you can't hook a filter onto a hand pump, we could only use the water for washing dishes and such. It is best to place the hand pump in a bucket of water for one or two hours before you use it. This allows the leather seal to expand and seal properly. You will also need to prime the pump before you can get water up. To prime it just pour water in through the top of the pump. The water will come out dirty on a newly driven well for the first day or two.

Later on, we decided to put in an electric pump. Sears had the least expensive pump I could find. Sampson Hardware has a nice 4½ gallon (17 liter) pressure tank at a low price. You will need a pressure tank. Even a small one helps to keep the water pressure constant and the pump primed. The pump will overheat due to constantly turning off and on if it does not have the pressure tank. From the pump I ran a pipe to a "T" divider. One direction from the "T", the pipe goes into a whole house type filter; from there it would go into a water softer if we had one. Next, on our first temporary setup, the water went into a 3/8th inch (9.5 mm) flexible copper tubing to the sink. The other direction from the "T" went to a water faucet outside. I also installed a cutoff valve inside the house so water wouldn't freeze up in the faucet outside as I could open and drain the outside faucet. Latter still I installed a water heater and a temporary shower hooked up with 3/8th inch (9.5 mm) flexible copper tubing. When I finished out the house with sheet rocked walls, I used the standard rigid copper tubing which I considered to be more reliable in freezing temperatures than CPVC plastic pipe. CPVC plastic pipe is easier to install and should be used if the well water is too acidic of which a lot of Alaskan water is. Soft copper pipe is sized by its outside diameter whereas rigid copper pipe is sized by its interior diameter. For plumbing installation instruction I recommend the Home Depot book "Plumbing 1-2-3". I also used the Home Depot book "Home Improvement 1-2-3" which covers many construction projects needed to complete and finish out the house as well. Both books give good step by step instructions along with pictures for soldering copper pipes and installing various plumbing fixtures like sinks, showers, toilets, etc. I am not a licensed plumber or electrician so I defer to these books which I used and found to give enough "how to" information to make the work go smoothly and function properly and safely along with good step by step pictures.

Trying out the well

13 WOODSTOVE, WOODSHED, HEATING OIL FURNACE

Two of the most important things to have in Alaska, or any cold climate area, are a good wood stove and a woodshed. There are a few things to look for in a good wood stove. A good wood stove will be air tight. An air tight stove has welded seams and a fiberglass gasket around the door to seal out the air. The stove gets its air through two air vents which can be adjusted by screwing them in or out or pushing a lever on some brands of stoves. When the air vents are closed all the way, then no air gets to the fire and it goes out. A good stove will also have bricks inside on which you lay the wood. A grate is not used at all. The bricks protect the stove from getting a burned out bottom. Another good thing to have is a spring shaped stainless steel door handle because it remains cool to the touch. I like having a window in order to see the fire burn. It not only makes the house cozier but also lets you see how the fire is doing at a glance. I clean the chimney once a month and the fireplace ashes every week when it is being used a lot. Use a water spray bottle to reduce the ash dust as you clean out the fire place.

You will need to install a chimney and a fire proof pad for your fireplace. Since the fire place is so heavy, the floor will need to have some extra support underneath it. An extra pier or some pilings from the ground up to and supporting two of the joists on which the fireplace will sit should do the job. It is best to tend to all this before placing the joist down. The fire and heat resistant platform I used under my fireplace was in three layers. First, above the floor I put a special metal-covered insulated material. You can get this at most places that sell wood stoves. Above this, place a layer of 15½ by 7½ by 1½ inch (39 by 19 by 3.8 cm) bricks. Above the bricks I put a sheet of metal. Make sure you cut off the sharp corners and file off all the burrs. After figuring out where the chimney is to connect to the fireplace, make a hole above this location through the roof. I used my .22 caliber (0.056 mm) semi-automatic rifle to shoot a circular hole through the roof of the proper diameter. I figured that there was not much left of the bullets after going through the plywood and tin, but it probably would not be a good idea to do if other people are around for the bullets to fall back down on. I did not have electricity to use an electric drill at that time. I then cleaned up the rough edges with sheet metal cutting shears. Next place the woodstove in place and start up with the chimney. Where the chimney goes through the beams, you will need to use insulated pipe the rest or the way up through the roof. At this junction at the beams, connect a fire block chimney support to the two beams it goes through. Continue with the chimney pipe on up through the roof to a height above the roof recommended by the manufacturer (usually chimneys must extend a minimum of 3 feet (1 m) above the roof surface and 2 feet (0.61 m) higher than any part of the building within 10 feet (3 m)). It has been my experience that if the chimney is higher than the roof peak, then it should be high enough. Don't get it too high to reach for cleaning out. It should be swept out once a month in below zero temperatures to prevent chimney fires. The creosote builds up quicker in cold temperatures when you use the woodstove a lot and when you turn the air intake down at night. Stuff some fiberglass insulation and then cover with caulk around where the chimney goes through the roof. Add the metal flashing around the chimney on the roof and caulk around it as well. Now, just cap the top of the chimney.

A woodshed not only keeps the snow off your wood but also helps it to dry out faster during the summer. A woodshed is simple to build should be covered with tin. Our 1¾ acres (7082 m²) of land had enough trees to build our 13 by 41 foot (3.96 by 12.5 m) cabin, the 8 by 28 foot (2.44 by 8.5 m) add on, the frame for 1 storage building, 2 woodsheds, and the frame for the outhouse. Additionally, we had enough trees on our land to supply us in fire wood for three years and one half years.

After three years of using a woodstove for our heat, I got a heating oil (diesel) furnace. I bought a very energy efficient Toyostove Laser 73 Kerosene Heating System. For less cold climates a smaller model Toyostove will work fine. Instead of kerosene, I used the much less expensive heating oil (diesel) #1. You cannot use standard #2 diesel. The Toyostove uses a two way pipe to both exhaust the exhaust gases out and suck in fresh, pre-heated, air to burn. You will need to cut a small, about three inch diameter, hole through the wall for this to go through. Included in this pipe that goes through this hole is an insulated pipe to protect the wall from getting hot and catching on fire. I bought a 500 gallon (1893 liter) above ground tank to store the diesel in. About 400 to 450 gallons (1514 to 1703 liters) would last me for the entire winter season. I installed a cut off and filter at the tank discharge, then ran a 3/8th (9.5 mm) flexible copper tubing line underground to the house then through the wall and connected it to the stove. The woodstove is nice, historic, romantic, etc., but the ash (dust) free, constant temperature easiness of the oil furnace; along with freeing summer time up to fish instead of gathering firewood has to be considered. A woodstove is a must for a backup just in case you lose power or run out of fuel.

Woodshed

Oil furnace

14 SEPTIC TANK AND LEACH FIELD

If you cannot connect to the city's sewer system and you use a flush toilet, then you will need a septic tank and leach field to process the sewer. A 1000 gallon (3785 liter) septic tank is considered the minimum size for most locations. Two 500 gallon (1893 liter) tanks can be used side by side to aid in handling the weight during installation. For a weekend cabin, a 500 gallon (1893 liter) tank is considered adequate. I used a 500 gallon (1893 liter) plastic septic tank on which I had sprayed 3 inches (7.6 cm) of foam insulation to help keep the septic tanks' water warm. The warm septic tank is supposed to allow bacteria to break down solid materials before they go out of the septic tank and into the leach field to be absorbed by the soil. Generally, the following distances should be considered for the placement area of the leach field as far as minimum distances from certain objects: water well (100 feet (30 m)), building (10 feet (3 m)), stream, pond or lake (75 to 100 feet

(23 to 30 m)), septic tank (5 feet (1.5 m)). The size of the leach field depends on how much water will be going through it and the ability of the soil at 5 feet (1.5 m) down to absorb it. The old standard was 150 gallons (568 liters) a day per bedroom was to be expected. Water saving toilets and showers use less water today. In general, on well-draining gravel or sand, a 700 square foot (65 square meter) leach field should work. With these sizes in mind, pick your spot for where the septic tank and leach field are to go. I picked an area clear of trees to put mine. The drain pipes are typically 10 feet (3 m) long with holes cut on two sides along its length.

I put in the septic tank first with a temporary leach field going into three 55 gallon (208 liter) metal barrels shot through with holes to allow the water to drain out. I used a shovel and hand dug the hole for the septic tank. I was planning on using the temporary leach field for several years before digging a proper one, but I did not put a filter cloth on top of it and the silt type soil that I covered it with, along with the silt type soil that was mixed in with the gravel, stopped up the ability of the water to drain into the soil. When this occurred, sewer water started coming up to the surface of the ground. So after just one year I needed to put in a proper leach drain field.

I rented a backhoe loader to dig the hole for my leach field. I wanted to rent it for just one day and, without a trailer to haul the backhoe on, I had to drive it to my place which took about three hours. Again I wanted to finish and return the backhoe in a 24 hour period to save money. With the long day light hours in Alaska's interior during the summer, I was able to work all night long. I had already had one dump truck load of coarse rocks delivered to my property and was ready to be used. I dug the hole for the leach field starting near the septic tank and working my way away from it. Using the loader, I dumped the coarse rocks on one end of the leach field. My wife and I used a wheel barrow and shovels to spread the rocks out. I then installed the perforated leach field pipe into the leach field in three rolls that I joined together in like manner on the other end. The drain piping was thus three rolls of piping extending 40 feet (12 m) and being 20 feet (6 m) wide. I connected the leach field pipes to the septic tank with sewer black ABS pipe and the cement glue made to join it. While doing this, I installed a clean out that would be above the ground surface and come down and join the ABS pipe. I covered the pipes with filter cloth which allows water to filter through but keeps silt from going through. I then used the loader portion of the backhoe to cover the perforated pipes up. Instead of the cloth filter cloth, some now use a curved plastic (half circle or upside down "U" shaped) enclosure. These have no bottom and have downward slanting holes on the sides, but not on the top. Thus sewer water drains at the bottom and sides while the top keeps the top soil silt out. No stone or filter cloth is required. They must be buried at least 1 foot (0.3 m) down but no more than 3 feet (1 m) down, to keep the weight of the soil from crushing it, depending on the manufacturers' instructions. Now days it is recommended to use a junction box between the septic tank and the leach field. The junction box has one 4 inch (10 cm) pipe entering the box from the septic tank and, for my leach field, three sewer pipes leaving it and going to the perforated sewer pipes. If you use the "U" shaped gravel-less plastic leaching chambers, it would be better to dig 3 feet (1 m) wide trenches instead of one pit for the leach field.

Working on the septic system

Working on the leach field

15   FINISHING UP AND HELPFUL IDEAS

The cabin is now nearly complete; at least the hardest work is over. Now comes several, comparatively speaking, little jobs which need to be done. For the most part you can do the following jobs in any order.

A vinyl type floor helps to protect the floor from water, especially in the kitchen and entry ways. If ease of use is important I recommend using the type of vinyl that you simply roll out and nail down at the edges. I used the type that you glue down to the floor for its entirety. I installed the floor covering over the entire cabins' floor and nailed the inside partition wall boards down on top of the vinyl flooring. This is a lot easier than having to cut the flooring to fit each room. The place where you buy it can let you know all of your options for the type of flooring you choose to use.

You can install the electric wires for the house yourself if you follow the standard wiring instructions from an electrical book. Also check for any code books particular to your county, borough, or city. The library is a good source for these books as well as hardware stores. I like Black & Decker's "The Complete Guide to Home Wiring". I am not a licensed plumber or electrician so I defer to these books which I used and found to give enough "how to" information to make the work go smoothly and function properly and safely along with good step by step pictures. Electric wires and connections installed improperly or of the wrong size (gauge) can cause fires and shock and kill you. Be careful not to connect the black hot wire to a connection that is made for the white neutral wire. It will work either way but can give someone an unexpected shock in the future while working on it for some reason. If the hot and neutral wires are switched at the switch connection, the switch will not turn the current supply off to the plug or light (even though it will not be on or running due to the neutral wire being open when the switch is in the off position). When someone touches it the current will use them as a ground. Phone installation is easy to do also and is covered in the Black & Decker book as well. Wiring in your cabin is easy; there is nothing hard to understand about it if you have a good book to go by and are careful. If you are in the city limits, they probably have rules which allow only licensed electricians to do such work, along with a permit fee. That's another good reason not to build in the city. I stapled 12 gauge (2.32 mm) romex wires directly to the logs and nailed the plug and switch boxes to the logs as well. There are no exposed wires and this is completely safe. For people without electricity, propane gas lights work fairly well.

If you have electricity, then you can install a vent hood. Carefully cut a hole through the wall of the proper diameter with a chain saw. It is dangerous since the saw can kick up. Use some screws to hold together a support system of small logs to hold up the vent hood. The vent hood itself can then be fastened to these logs with screws. I put up some metal roof flashing on the walls around the stove area to protect the walls from splattering grease.

To hang your clothes instead of using a closet or in addition to the closet, simply cut out some 3 or 4 feet (1 to 1.2 m) long sticks of about 1½ inch (3.8 cm) diameter and hang them from the beams with heavy string. To keep dust off your clothes, you can cover them with a bed sheet.

I made my upper kitchen cabinet out of ¾ inch (1.9 cm) plywood and 1 x 2 inch (2.5 x 5 cm) boards. It wasn't too hard to do, but I should have used a square to check my work more instead of just eyeing it to have square corners. I attached the cabinet to the wall logs by using 3 screws through a 1 x 4 inch (2.54 x 10.2 cm) board that I put inside the cabinet going across the top, back part of the cabinet. I also built some bookshelves / storage shelves in the add-on out of 1 x 10 inch (2.5 x 25.4 cm) finished (dimensional) lumber and finish nails. I staggered the height position of each neighboring shelf in order to have a place to nail the shelf to the vertical 1 x 10 inch (2.5 x 25.4 cm) boards. I used thin ¼ inch (6 mm) plywood for the backing.

At first we did not have a septic tank sewage system. So our used sink and tub water drained into a five gallon bucket, which I hauled outside and dumped. I raised the tub up high enough so that a five gallon bucket (latter I used a big industrial mop bucket on wheels) could sit below the drain. For the stand of the tub I nailed two 1 by 4 inch (2.5 by 10 cm) boards along the sides of three 6 by 6 inch (15 by 15 cm) pieces of lumber stacked on top of each other. I made two sets of these to set the tub on. I nailed a 2 by 4 inch (5 by 10 cm) board to the front and back side of where the tub is to sit. And to ensure strength, I drilled a ½ inch (12.7 mm) hole through all three 6 by 6 inch (15 by 15 cm) pieces of lumber and drove rebar down through them to keep them together. I put up plastic sheeting around the two ends and back side of the tub. On the front side of the tub I tied the two ends of a regular shower curtain rod with copper wire onto two beams. Then I put a regular shower curtain on it. We used the campout type shower bag to take a shower with. I rigged a double pulley system with some small cord to make it easier to lift up the water bag after filling it with water.

An outhouse type toilet is fine for warm weather, but it is too cold during the winter. For our toilet we first used a bedside handicap toilet. We put trash bags in it each time we needed to use it. I did build an outhouse by first digging a hole and then putting a metal 55 gallon (208 liter) barrel down into the hole. I first shot (or you can drill) holes into the bottom of the barrel. For the base of the outhouse I used 6 x 6 inch (15 x 15 cm) lumber around the edges and around the barrel hole to give support to the plywood board that I used for the floor. I used four vertical post logs for the frame which were held together at the top by four horizontal logs each toe nailed to the vertical post logs. I used ½ inch (12.7 mm) plywood to make the walls and roof and door of the outhouse. The roof should extend out 12 inches (30 cm) in the front and rear and about 3 inches (7.6 cm) on the sides to keep rain water off. I simply used a jig saw and cut the door out of the piece of plywood that was used for the front of the outhouse and then put hinges and a small dead bolt type lock on it. For the door handle I put a screw from the inside of the plywood door into a small 2 x 2 x 2 inch (5 x 5 x 5 cm) board on the outside. I drilled several 1 inch (2.5 cm) diameter holes on both sides and cut out a crescent moon on the door for ventilation. I tacked some screen material over the holes to keep the bugs out.

There are several options for walls to make bedroom divisions. You can use logs or do it the standard way with 2 by 4 inch (5 by 10 cm) boards and sheet rock. 2 x 4 inch (5 by 10 cm) boards and sheet rock works best for having an out of the way place to run the plumbing (hot and cold water supply and plastic drain and vent pipe) and electric wiring. For plumbing installation instruction I recommend the Home Depot book "Plumbing 1-2-3". It not only covers supply and drain pipe installation instructions, but also sink, tub and toilet as well. For wiring installation instruction I recommend the Black & Decker book "The complete guide to Home Wiring". I also used the Home Depot book "Home Improvement 1-2-3" which covers many construction projects needed to complete the house including room framing and installing sheetrock. Again, I am not a licensed plumber or electrician so I defer to these books which I used and found to give enough "how to" information to make the work go smoothly and function properly and safely along with good step by step pictures. Temporarily I used ½ inch (12.7 mm) plywood for inside partition walls at first. To hold the plywood steady at the bottom I nailed a 1 by 1 inch (2.5 by 2.5 cm) board along the bottom to the floor and nailed the plywood into it. And at each vertical edge of the plywood where each piece came together, I nailed on a 2 by 4 inch (5 by 10 cm) board. I nailed the 2 by 4 inch (5 by 10 cm) board into the beam itself for stability. I thought it might give me trouble when the roof got heavy with snow, but it didn't flex down any that I could tell. For a temporarily door to the bedrooms you can hang a bed sheet or shower curtain. When I finished the house with sheetrock walls, I used closet type folding doors for the restroom and the hallway bedroom to prevent the door from being in the way. I used louvered doors for the closet to keep it vented and dry.

If you have a vehicle then you will have to deal with removing snow from your driveway. I had to remove snow from my house to a little over ¼ of a mile (0.4 km) to the road. During our first winter I pulled a "V" shaped plow made out of logs and 2 by 6 inch (5 by 10 cm) boards behind my truck. I later added about 2 feet (0.61 m) high plywood to the sides to raise the sides up to better plow the snow. This worked good for the first 30 to 40 inches (0.76 to 1 m) of snow, but after that the plow couldn't throw the snow up over the wall of snow beside the road. So I had to go back through with a shovel and shovel the sides clear. This was hard work and took a lot of time. Then we got a 5 horsepower snow thrower. It is a lot easier and only takes about two to three hours depending on how much snow there is to be removed. I think the best way of clearing snow is to use a plow on the front of a four wheel drive truck. It cost a lot more than a snow thrower, but works faster and can provide a source of income by doing other people's driveways. After removing the snow by the "V" plow or snow thrower, I would drive back and forth along the drive way road covering a different area of the road with my tires each time thus packing down any leftover snow. A hard packed snow road will be less likely to get you stuck. During the spring melt, I was able to drive on the melting hard pack as it melted away without getting stuck.

Snow plow to be pulled behind truck

Snow thrower

Homemade kitchen cabinets

Homemade kitchen cabinets

Homemade book / storage shelves in add-on

The finished cabin kitchen area. (Note the water distiller used to purify drinking water until I installed a reverse osmosis system).

The finished cabin

The finished cabin: shower

The finished cabin: restroom sink

The finished cabin: front

Note that the pipe coming out of the log below the window is the exhaust pipe for the Toyostove & the insulated pipe coming up from the ground is the diesel supply line.

The finished cabin: side opposite of add-on

16 BUILDING A PERGOLA PATIO COVER

A pergola type patio cover gives a patio sitting area a fresh woodsy outdoorsy character without the closed in feeling that a regular covered cover patio has. A pergola is best made of rough cedar and left unpainted. The pergola has a crisscross of cross beams that give some shade as is, but also supports vine type plants such as the wisteria or grapevines thus giving more shade as well as garden color. It will bring your outdoor patio area to life. They have been around a long time and were common in Italian Renaissance gardens. I recommend using rough red wood cedar lumber to build your pergola. Red wood cedar contains plicatic acid which is part of the reason that the wood is so very rot resistant. The saw dust can cause an allergic asthma reaction in some people. Don't chew on a wood chip because the wet cedar wood chip will get the plicatic acid on you. Like poison ivy, it is slow to heal. Surprisingly, handling the wood and even splinters from it does not cause any problems in most people.

The most common size pergola is either 10 by 12 feet (3 by 3.66 m) or 12 by 12 feet (3.66 by 3.66 m). The inside walls on that side of my house are 10 feet (3 m) high instead of the common 8 feet (2.44 m); therefore my house was high enough to connect the pergola to. I connected one side of my pergola to my house which eliminated the need for two of the post and two beams (some people call these beams headers, and the ledger board that connects to the house some call a header board as well since it heads up the joist ends). If you do not connect the pergola to your house, you will need two more post and two more double beams. Additionally, for stability, you will need double beams running in the opposite direction on both sides below the double beams that are there. That is to say running below and perpendicular to the double beams just mentioned. A single beam can be used but it lacks in eye appeal to match the other double beams and for the rugged strong look. My pergola extends 10 feet (3.1 m) from my house and is 12 feet (3.66 m) wide. I used three 2" x 8" x 12' (5 x 20 cm x 3.66 m) boards (one as a ledger board and two for beams), eleven 2" x 8" x 10' (5 x 20 cm x 3.1 m) joist boards placed about 12 inches (30.5 cm) on center, and eighteen 2" x 4" x 12' (5 x 10 cm x 3.66 m) strapping boards (some call them stringers since they connect the joist together) placed 5¼ inches (13.3 cm) on center. It is best to use 2" x 2" (5 x 5 cm) instcad of 2" x 4" (5 x 10 cm) boards, but I wanted a little more shade. I also used two 6" x 6" x 12' (15 x 15 cm x 3.66 m) post which I cut off 2 feet (0.61 m) to meet the needs of the height of my pergola. The spacing between joists can vary from 12" to 24" (30 to 60 cm) on center depending on what you want. Likewise, the spacing of the strapping boards can vary from 4" to 8" (10 to 20 cm) and look good.

The first thing to do is pick the location of where you want the pergola to be. Use a tape measure and see if the 12 x 12' or 12 x 10' (3.66 x 3.66 or 3.66 x 3.1 m) measurements will work there. Double check your measurements and step back to see if that is where you want it to be. Keep in mind blocking the sun rays, and the direction that the sun moves across the sky.

I picked my location where I wanted to build my pergola and set up my two 6" x 6" x 10' (15 x 15 x 3.1 m) post at 10 feet, 6 inches (3.2 m) on center apart from each other. This allows for the 12 feet (3.66 m) long double beam boards to stick out a little on each end. Nail two 2" x 4" x 8' (5 x 10 cm x 2.44 m) temporary boards at 90 degrees from each other to support and hold the post in place. Use one nail into the post about four or five feet up on one end and place one nail into a short spike board that is driven into the ground on the other end. I secured the base to the cement by using a 90 degree angled metal strip that has four holes in it. I drilled two holes into the cement with a 3/8 inch (9.5 mm) masonry drill bit. I then tightened down two 3/8 inch (9.5 mm) by 2¼ inch (5.7 cm) wedge anchors securing the bottom of the 90 degree angled metal strip. Through the other two holes I screwed two 5/16th inch by 4 inches long (8 mm by 10 cm) coarse-thread lag bolt screws. I used an electric drill to drive the screws into the wood instead of a hand held screw driver. If you do not connect to the house on one side, then you will need to set up the other two posts as well. You can install the 2" x 8" x 12' (5 x 20 cm x 3.66 m) beams first before the next two post, but I recommend waiting until the ledger board is installed.

Next, connect a 2" x 8" x 12' (5 x 20 x 3.66 m) ledger board (header) to the house so that it runs parallel to the two post. My house has a non-structural fascia board where I needed to connect the header. Behind the fascia board is a 1" x 4" (2.5 x 10 cm) board which is nailed to 2" x 6" (5 x 15 cm) roof rafters spaced 24"

(55.88 cm) on center. I removed the soffit vents so I could determine exactly where the rafters butted up to the 1" x 4" (2.5 x 10 cm) board. If you do not have enough soffit vents there, add them. Mark on the fascia board the center of each rafter. Measure these distances and mark the same on the ledger board. Also mark on the fascia board the place where the ledger board's end will start. Pre start into the ledger board the 5/16" x 5" to 6" (8 mm x 13 to 15 cm) coarse-thread lag screw bolts to line up to where the rafters will be. Since I had to place the screw bolts just one inch from the top edge of the ledger board to be able to connect to the rafter, I also used several 8 inch (20 cm) long by 1 inch (2.5 cm) wide mending plates which have three other holes for screws in them to insure the ledger board did not split after it received the weight of the joist and strapping boards. I screwed 5/16" x 1½" (8 mm x 1.3 cm) coarse-thread lag screw bolts into the other three holes in the mending plates. It helps to have someone help you hold the 12 foot (3.66 m) long header in place as you use a drill with a star tool insert to drive the screw bolts into the rafter boards. Next, add the eleven joist hangers spaced 12" (30 cm) on center as I did or use up to 24" (60 cm) on center and less joist boards if you choose to. Start the first one 6" (15 cm) from the edge of the ledger board.

Next, measure the distance from the cement up to the bottom of the ledger board that is connected to the house. Mark this same distance up on the two posts. Above this mark is where the two 2" x 8" x 12' (5 x 20 cm x 3.66 m) beams will go. But first make any decorative end cuts before installing them.

You do not have to have any decorative end cuts to the beams and joist, you can leave them square if you wish, but I prefer a 45 degree end cut. To do this, using a square, measure 3 to 4 inches (7.6-10 cm) in both directions from the bottom edge of the beams and the joists and make a mark. Draw a line between your two marks and cut with a skill hand saw along the line.

Now you are ready to place the 2" x 8" x 10' (5 x 20 cm x 3.1 m) joist into the joist hangers on one end and across the beams on the other end. Measure and mark the same distances between the joist hangers on top of one of the beams. Place a joist on top of the beam and into the joist hanger and secure both ends. Joist hangers have holes to drive nails or screw screws through into the joists. Toe nail the joist into the beams on the other end with galvanized 10d 3" (7.6 cm) nails. Joist hangers are made for dimensional cut wood of 1½ inch (3.8 cm) width. The 2 inch (5 cm) rough cut cedar boards are 1¾ inch (4.4 cm) width. While someone holds the joist in the joist hanger, on the other end, beat a scrap 2 x 4" (5 x 10 cm) board with a heavy hammer to push the joist into the narrow joist hanger.

If you connect the pergola to the house, nail a 6" (15 cm) or so sheet of aluminum or galvanized flashing on top of the joist where the joist meets the house to keep water out of the area where the ledger board connects to the facial board. Use aluminum or galvanized roofing nails. I also caulked this area for added protection.

Next mark the tops of the two outside end joist for where the strapping boards will go (I used about 5¼" (13 cm) on center) and started back from the joist ends about 7" (18 cm). Nail one galvanized 10d 3" (7.6 cm) nail into each strapping board on the outside joist, and then do the same on the opposite side outside joist. Next nail one nail into the strapping boards where they go over each joist throughout the pergola. I used silicone caulk on top of these nails to further prevent the chance of rust stains in the future.

You are now finished with the pergola construction. You can add a vine type plant at the base of the two posts if you wish. If the sun is a problem on one side or area you can add outdoor blinds that can be rolled up or let down as needed. You can also build a more permanent blind that connects between the two posts and goes down to about three or four feet above the ground using a wicker type privacy lattice. You might want to hang a bench swing between the two posts. Sit back and enjoy your pergola patio area with the added satisfaction that you built it yourself.

Temporary post supports. Note the boards standing in the left portion of the picture. I first tried putting all of the joist boards together and lifting them up and installing them as a unit but it was too heavy for two men to lift and install alone.

Anchor post to cement

Decorative cut

Joist to header

Joist to header

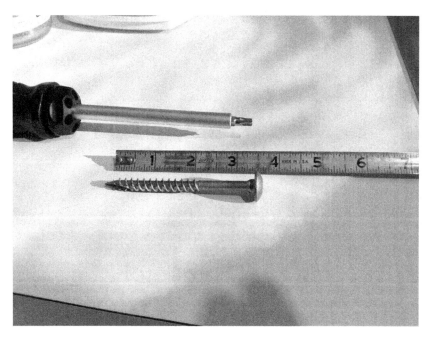

Lag screw (comes in different lengths)

Looking away from house

The finished pergola

The finished pergola & Woody (2011)

FROM THE AUTHOR

I built the log cabin in 1992 and the add-on in 1993. My first trip to Alaska was in 1981. At 20 years of age I drove up to Alaska from Texas to prospect for gold and find adventure. I fell in love with Alaska. I wrote about that experience in a book: THE WILD STILL CALLS TO ALASKA: Looking for gold; enjoying the wild! The book is available in print and eBook formats:

THE WILD STILL CALLS TO ALASKA: Looking for gold; enjoying the wild!

By Charles (Woody) Underwood

ISBN: 9781495217258 (Print)

ISBN: 9780615951713 (eBook)

Book description: It is the story about two men who travel to Alaska from Texas to go out into Alaska's wilderness prospecting for gold and looking for adventure. After arriving in Fairbanks, before departing on the bush plane, Woody's friend changes his mind about going. Woody continues on alone into the Alaskan wilderness in 1981. It would be going into new territories, with new experiences, and a lot of adventure traveling more than 1564 miles (2517 km) across Alaska. Starting from Fairbanks and going to Kotzebue, Buckland, Nome, Resurrection Creek by Hope, and Salcha.

***

Made in the USA
Middletown, DE
12 December 2020